A HANDBOOK OF

MUSICAL KNOWLEDGE

A HANDBOOK OF MUSICAL KNOWLEDGE

BY

JAMES MURRAY BROWN

D.MUS., HON. FTCL, LRAM

PUBLISHED BY

TRINITY COLLEGE LONDON

89 ALBERT EMBANKMENT, LONDON SE1 7TP, UK

TRINITY COLLEGE LONDON

89 Albert Embankment

London SE1 7TP, UK

First Published 1967

Revised and Complete Edition 1987

CONTENTS

INTRODUCTION

When this book was first published in 1967, the material contained in its eight chapters related specifically to the content of the Grade One to Eight Theory of Music written examinations of Trinity College. This revised edition takes into account most of the changes which have been introduced more recently in those examinations, but may not match their content in every aspect. It is now offered as a general text book on the subject, in the hope that students preparing for any theory of music examinations will find it helpful. Students are advised to master each chapter thoroughly before passing on to the next.

It is recommended that when using this book teachers and students should play all examples, on the piano, to ensure that the theory of music is studied with the aim of appreciating its *sound* and understanding *why* it sounds as it does.

JMB 1987

Chapter I

1. Musical notes have PITCH, DURATION and INTENSITY. The first two qualities are the only ones that need concern us at present.

PITCH

2. If you sit at the piano facing the keyboard, the notes to your right are the high ones and those to your left the low ones, thus:

These notes are given letter names ascending from A to G and these are repeated as the pattern of notes is repeated, thus:

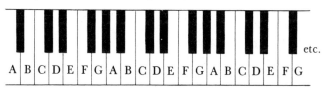

Notice the position of the letter names in relation to the grouping of the black notes.

3. The notes nearest to one another that have the same letter name are said to be an OCTAVE away from one another.

4. To indicate their pitch, notes are written on a stave of five lines. The notes can be written on the lines or in the spaces between the lines and are reckoned from the lowest one upwards, low on the stave corresponding to low or bass on the keyboard:

lines _____ spaces _____

5. To relate this stave to the pitch of notes accurately, a sign called a CLEF is used to fix the position of certain letter names on it. Two clefs are commonly used, one for the high notes—the G or treble clef, the other for the low notes—the F or bass clef.

6. The treble clef, originally resembling a capital G, fixes the second line as the note G just to the right of the middle of the keyboard:

7. The bass clef fixes the fourth line as the note F just to the left of the middle of the keyboard. Note the two forms and the position of the two dots one on each side of the F line:

8.   Thus the notes on the treble stave are:

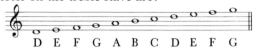

D   E   F   G   A   B   C   D   E   F   G

9.   And the notes on the bass stave are:

F   G   A   B   C   D   E   F   G   A   B

10.   The range of sounds used in music goes beyond these two staves and notes that are beyond them are put on extra short lines or between them in the spaces formed by them. These short lines are called LEGER lines, thus:

11.   The note on the leger line below the treble stave is the same as the note on the leger line above the bass stave and is known as MIDDLE C, being the C nearest the middle of the keyboard.

   Thus the full range of our notes allowing one leger line above and one below each stave is:

D   E   F   G   A   B   C   D   E   F   G   A   B   C   D

12.   A SEMITONE is the distance between two adjacent notes, whether black or white, but some white notes have black ones between them. Thus there are semitones between all the E's and F's, and between all the B's and C's, and also between any note and its adjacent black notes.

13.   Two semitones form one TONE or WHOLE-TONE. Thus there are tones between the C's and the D's for example, and between the D's and the E's, etc.

14.   The sign ♯ is a SHARP and it raises the note that comes immediately after it one semitone:

which is the black note between G and A.

15. The sign ♭ is a FLAT and lowers a note one semitone, thus:

which again is a black note between G and F.
Note the exact position of the sharp and the flat on the stave relative to the note inflected.

16. Notice that on the piano B sharp is the same as C
    C flat is the same as B
    E sharp is the same as F
    F flat is the same as E

17. The sign ♮ is a NATURAL and cancels a flat or a sharp, thus:

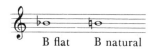

The flat and sharp and natural signs are called ACCIDENTALS and only inflect the note against which they are written, not those bearing the same letter name in another octave.

DURATION

18. In written music, the length of a note is shown by its shape.

19. When there is no note sounding, a REST is written and the length of the rest is also shown by its shape.

20. Here is a table showing the relative lengths of notes and the corresponding rests:

NAME	SIGN	VALUE COMPARED TO o	REST
SEMIBREVE	o		▬
MINIM	𝅗𝅥	$\frac{1}{2}$ o	▬
CROTCHET	𝅘𝅥	$\frac{1}{4}$ o	⸙ or ⌐
QUAVER	𝅘𝅥𝅮	$\frac{1}{8}$ o	𝄾

There are others but they need not concern us at present.

21. The minim is like a semibreve with a stem or tail attached. Notice that when the minim is above the middle line of the stave the stem is written downwards from the left hand side of the note, while if the note is below the middle line of the stave the stem is written upwards from the right hand side of the note, thus:

If the note is on the middle line the stem may be written up or down as convenient.

TIME

22.   Our normal music has a regular pulse or throb. These pulses are called BEATS.

23.   These beats generally fall into regular groups because some are accented and some are not. In these examples the sign $>$ indicates a note that is naturally more accented than others:

24.   In writing music the strongest of these accents are normally indicated by putting a line vertically across the stave *in front* of them. These lines are called BAR LINES:

25.   These lines divide the music into equal measures which are called BARS.

26.   The end of a piece of music is marked by two vertical lines known as the DOUBLE BAR:

27.   The regular grouping of beats into bars is called the TIME of the music and the kind of time depending on whether the accents occur in twos, threes or fours is indicated by a TIME SIGNATURE written on the stave after the clef at the beginning of the piece.
   If the beats fall into regular groups of two we say it is in DUPLE time and we write the figure 2 as the top number of the time signature.
   Similarly if the beats fall into groups of three we call it TRIPLE time and write a 3 as the top figure of the time signature.
   Groups of beats in fours are called QUADRUPLE time and the top figure of the time signature will be 4.

28.   Thus the top figure of the time signature indicates the number of beats in the bar.

29.   The bottom figure however indicates the length of the note that constitutes each beat expressed in fractions of a semibreve. The whole time signature thus resembles a fraction in arithmetic.

   $\frac{3}{4}$ indicates three crotchet beats in a bar, since a crotchet is one quarter of a semibreve. This is triple time.

   $\frac{2}{4}$ indicates two crotchet beats in a bar. This is duple time.

   $\frac{4}{4}$ indicates four crotchet beats in a bar. This is quadruple time.

30.   The $\frac{2}{2}$ time signature is often called ALLA BREVE, and may be indicated $\math163{C}$.

31. $\frac{4}{4}$ time is often called COMMON TIME and may be indicated thus—

C. The origin of this mode of notation of time dates back to medieval days when triple time was looked on as being connected with the Trinity and so was perfect and indicated by a circle— O, while duple time, the imperfect time, was indicated by a half circle— C.

32. When a note is inflected by an accidental, it is so inflected until the end of the bar in which it appears unless it is cancelled before the bar line.

RHYTHM and GROUPING of NOTES

33. In so far as it is possible to do so, notes and rests should be grouped so as to show the position of the beats in a bar.

34. Tails of quavers should be joined to group them into beats:

35. These exceptions to the rule should be noted:

(a) In $\frac{4}{4}$, if beats one and two, or beats three and four consist of quavers, they should be joined:

(b) In $\frac{4}{4}$, if the middle *note* is a minim it may be so written:

thus  is

correct but if the middle of the bar is a *rest* lasting a minim, the individual beat rests must be shown:

Also notice that if a bar of $\frac{3}{4}$ consists of a crotchet and then rests on beats two and three, the two rest beats must be shown as two crotchet rests, not as a minim one:

but if the second and third beats are one note, a minim may be used:

(c) In $\frac{2}{4}$, the four quavers, when they occur in a bar, should have their tails joined:

(d) In $\frac{3}{4}$, a bar consisting of six quavers should all have their tails joined:

(f) In $\frac{4}{4}$, a rest for the duration of the first two beats or for beats three and four may be written as a minim rest:

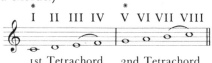

THE MAJOR SCALE

36. If the note C is played on the piano and the other white notes are played in succession until the next C is reached, the succession of notes is called the MAJOR SCALE. Not all the gaps between the notes are the same size, some being tones and some being semitones.

37. The eight notes of the major scale rising from C are divided into two groups known as TETRACHORDS, each of which contains four notes: (The word tetrachord is derived from two Greek words meaning four strings or notes—tetra and chorde.)

I   II   III   IV   V   VI   VII   VIII

1st Tetrachord   2nd Tetrachord

38. In the key of C, the note C is called Doh, Tonic or I. The fifth note of the scale will be G. This is known as Soh, the Dominant or V.

The scale above has these notes marked *.

Notice the numbering of the notes.

Notice also that the first Tetrachord commences on the Tonic (I) and the second on the Dominant (V).

39. Notice that the semitones lie in the same places in both tetrachords. These semitones are marked with a slur (⁀) in the above example. The distance between the third and fourth notes, and between the seventh and eighth notes in all major scales are semitones.

40. If the second tetrachord of the scale of C major is taken as the first tetrachord of a major scale starting on G, and the second tetrachord of G's scale is added, then the scale pattern lies as follows:

1st Tetrachord   2nd Tetrachord

Notice that the second tetrachord has not got a semitone between its third and fourth notes (marked with a cross—X). To achieve this, a sharp is added before the note F, raising it a semitone:

41. To avoid writing this sharp every time it occurs in a piece which has G as its key note, a sharp is placed on the stave after the clef.

42. This is called the KEY SIGNATURE, and indicates that all the F's in the piece are sharpened unless one is cancelled by placing a natural sign (♮) in front of the individual note concerned.

The sharp on F in the key signature indicates that G is the key note of the scale:

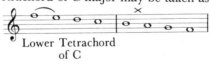

The key signature of a piece appears in the first bar of the piece immediately after the clef and before the time signature. The key signature is written on every line of the piece after the clef, whereas the time signature is only written at the beginning of the piece.

43. The bottom tetrachord of C major may be taken as the top tetrachord of a scale on F:

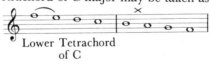

Lower Tetrachord
of C

But to preserve the shape in the lower tetrachord a flat has to be placed before the B:

This, like the sharp in G major will appear as the key signature of F major

44. This table shows the key signatures dealt with so far:

If the bass clef is used, they are written thus:

45.   Here are the major scales so far with the semitones marked with a slur:

MINOR SCALE

46.   The minor scale exists in two forms—the melodic form and the harmonic form. What really makes the scale minor is the minor third that appears above the tonic note. It will be seen that the third above A is C—a minor third.

47.   A minor has, like C major, no sharps or flats in its key signature. For this reason it is said to be related to it—A minor is the RELATIVE MINOR to C major, and C major is the RELATIVE MAJOR to A minor.

48.   Examination of the series of notes that make up the scale of A minor reveals that the arrangement of tones and half tones is not the same as it was in the major scale:

Nor do the two tetrachords match as they did in C major. Indeed the lack of similarity in the two tetrachords of the minor scale renders reference to the term tetrachord somewhat muddling.

49.   The term 'LAH MINOR' is often used for the minor scale in the tonic sol-fa system. It describes the position of the tonic of the minor scale in relation to the notes of the major scale.

The term TONIC MINOR relates to the minor scale on the same tonic as the major. Thus: C minor is the tonic minor of C major

A minor is the relative minor of C major

50.   In order to give a satisfactory leading note before the tonic in the rising minor scale, the seventh note G is sharpened. The reason for this will appear clearer later when we discuss cadences and harmony. So here is the complete scale of A minor:

This is known as the HARMONIC form since its notes are employed to build the chords used in the key of A minor. Note that from F to G♯ is greater than a whole tone, having three semitones. The interval is known as an AUGMENTED SECOND.

51.   The harmonic form is the same going up as coming down.

52.   Just as A minor is the relative minor of C major, so every major scale has a relative minor with the same key signature as its own and commencing on its sixth note (VI).

53.   Here are the Harmonic Minor Scales up to one sharp and one flat with their appropriate key signatures. Notice that the seventh degree of the scale is sharpened in the Harmonic Minor Scale.

A MINOR, RELATIVE TO C MAJOR—"HARMONIC FORM"

MINOR SCALE WITH SHARP—"HARMONIC FORM"

E minor, relative to G major.

MINOR SCALE WITH FLAT—"HARMONIC FORM"

D minor, relative to F major.

INTERVALS

54.   The distance in pitch between any two notes is called an INTERVAL. An interval that lies within the notes of an octave is called a simple interval. If the distance between the notes is greater than an octave it is called a compound interval. Thus the interval of a tenth is a compound third.

55.   When the two notes forming the interval are both to be found in the notes of the same key, the interval is said to be DIATONIC in that key.

56.   Intervals are counted by the number of diatonic notes contained in them, including both of them in the total.

Thus this interval: includes the notes E, F, G and A.

Therefore the interval is a fourth.

These notes: are C and D.

Therefore the interval is a second.

57. Intervals may be major, minor, augmented and diminished. At present we are only concerned with the intervals formed by the keynote (Tonic) with the other notes of the major and minor scales up to the fifth. Here are the intervals above the keynote of C major up to the fifth:

Here are those above the key note of A minor:

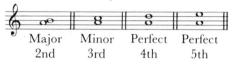

58. Perfect fourths, fifths and octaves are known as PERFECT CONCORDS.

59. Thirds and sixths are known as IMPERFECT CONCORDS.

60. Seconds and sevenths are DISCORDS.

61. Seconds, thirds, sixths and sevenths may be major or minor, depending on the number of semitones they contain. At present, we are only concerned with the intervals above the Tonic.
The major second contains two semitones.
The minor third contains three semitones.
The major third contains four semitones.
The perfect fourth contains five semitones.
The perfect fifth contains seven semitones.

CHORDS AND HARMONIC BEGINNINGS

62. A CHORD is a group of notes that are sounded together:

63. A TRIAD is a chord of three notes built on a note known as the ROOT, and consisting of root, the 3rd above it, and the 5th above it:

64. A triad may be built upon any note of the scale and if all its notes lie among the notes of any one key, it is a DIATONIC triad in that key; if they do not, it is a CHROMATIC triad. For the moment, only the former will be considered.

65. At present we are only concerned with the triads on I and V. Here they are in C major and D minor:

Notice that the third in the chord of V in the minor key is sharpened.

Chapter II

PITCH

66.   If it is desired to write the scale of C major for two octaves from middle C up or down, it will be seen that it is necessary to extend the number of leger lines used to *two* beyond the stave in each direction, thus:

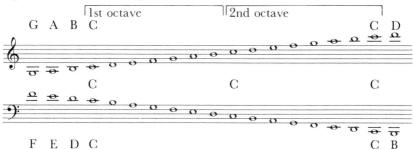

REWRITING A MELODY AT THE DISTANCE OF AN OCTAVE

67.   It will be a simple matter, if the note positions of a melody are known, to rewrite a melody in a different octave to the one in which it is written. Notice that if a note is in a space the note an octave above or below it will be on a line and vice versa:

68.   Therefore it is essential to know the positions of all the notes on the stave in both clefs.

DURATION

69.   The longest note in use is the breve and it is written thus: ‖ᴑ‖ . The breve is commonly used in the vocal music of the sixteenth and seventeenth centuries, but is unusual in later music.

70.   The rest which corresponds to it is ▆ This is only used in $\frac{4}{2}$ time.

71.   Notes shorter than the quaver are in common use.

A quaver $\left(\text{♪}\right)$ is equal to two semiquavers $\left(\text{♬}\right)$.

A semiquaver $\left(\text{♬}\right)$ is equal to two demisemiquavers $\left(\text{♬}\right)$.

72.   The rests which correspond to semiquaver and demisemiquaver are written thus: 𝄿 and 𝄿.

73. Here is a table showing the relative lengths of notes and the corresponding rests.

NAME	SIGN	VALUE COMPARED TO ❙◖❙ AND TO ◯	REST
BREVE	❙◖❙	— 2 × ◯	
SEMIBREVE	◯	$\frac{1}{2}$ ❙◖❙ and ◯	
MINIM	𝅗𝅥	$\frac{1}{4}$ ❙◖❙ and $\frac{1}{2}$ ◯	
CROTCHET	𝅘𝅥	$\frac{1}{8}$ ❙◖❙ and $\frac{1}{4}$ ◯	ⲣ or ⁄
QUAVER	𝅘𝅥𝅮	$\frac{1}{16}$ ❙◖❙ and $\frac{1}{8}$ ◯	
SEMIQUAVER	𝅘𝅥𝅯	$\frac{1}{32}$ ❙◖❙ and $\frac{1}{16}$ ◯	
DEMISEMIQUAVER	𝅘𝅥𝅰	$\frac{1}{64}$ ❙◖❙ and $\frac{1}{32}$ ◯	

Since the breve (❙◖❙) is seldom used nowadays, the longest normal note is the semibreve. In many places the names of the notes refer to their relationship to the semibreve, thus:

semibreve	—	whole note
minim	—	half note
crotchet	—	quarter note
quaver	—	eighth note
semiquaver	—	sixteenth note
demisemiquaver	—	thirtysecond note

74. N.B. A semibreve rest is used for a whole bar's rest in any time signature except $\frac{4}{2}$.

75. As with quavers, semiquavers and demisemiquavers have their tails joined so that they are grouped in beats:

76. Notes may be lengthened in two ways:
   (a) By tying a note to another note of the same pitch.
   (b) By putting a dot or dots after it.

77. Any number of notes may be tied together and this is indicated by joining them with a curved line, thus:

This method of extending the length is useful when a note is to be extended beyond the bar line.

78. Half the value of a note may be added to it by putting a dot after it, thus:

tied

Two dots may follow a note, in which case the note is lengthened by half its value and also by half the value added by the dot, thus:

tied

79. Rests are not tied together, but a rest may be lengthened by adding a dot or dots to it in the same way as notes are so lengthened.

80. Another way of adding to the length of a note or rest is by the placing of a pause mark ($\frown$) above or below the note or rest. This does not add an exact amount to a note as a dot or a tie does; it is left to the discretion of the performer how much is added.

81. A pause of unusual length over a rest or a note is sometimes marked "Lunga Pausa"; this is Italian for long pause.

82. A long curved line over a group of notes or a phrase is called a slur and indicates that the notes must be smoothly joined together:

83. The Italian word for smoothly is *legato*.

TIME

84. In considering time signatures, it is necessary to realise that the beat may not always be a crotchet. In other cases, the bottom figure will be 2 if a minim is the beat and 8 if a quaver is the beat. Thus:

$\frac{3}{2}$ indicates three minims in the bar.

$\frac{2}{2}$ indicates two minims in the bar.

$\frac{4}{2}$ indicates four minims in the bar.

The $\frac{2}{2}$ time signature is often called ALLA BREVE and may be indicated ₵, as is $\frac{4}{2}$.

85. The insertion of bar lines into a phrase of music when the time signature is given presents no problems. The notes will be grouped to indicate the beats and it is only necessary to count the beats in accordance with the time signature, thus:

barred

86. When no time signature is given, it is necessary to try to feel where the accents come and so find out whether it is duple, triple or quadruple time:

This melody presents obvious recurring accents on both of the C dotted crotchets and also on the C dotted minim. If only the first seven notes were given it would be possible to accent them thus:

A little unusual perhaps but perfectly possible. However the second half can only be accented thus:

The whole melody is thus obviously in triple time with the bar lines before the accents as under, and the first phrase will be found to conform to this time too, so that bars and time signature should be inserted thus:

since there is an accent every three crotchets; that is to say the time is three crotchets in the bar.

87. When bar lines are given it is only necessary to count the beats in order to add the time signature. But note this:

This melody could be either two minims in the bar or four crotchets in the bar, and time signatures of $\frac{2}{2}$, $\frac{4}{4}$, ¢ or C would all be equally correct. The duple time might be more likely if the minims were strongly accented at a fast pace, though no rule can be laid down over a point like this.

88. Here is the table of all the simple time signatures:

DUPLE	TRIPLE	QUADRUPLE
¢ or 2/2 ♩ ♩	3/2 ♩ ♩ ♩	¢ or 4/2 ♩ ♩ ♩ ♩
2/4 ♩ ♩	3/4 ♩ ♩ ♩	C or 4/4 ♩ ♩ ♩ ♩
2/8 ♪ ♪	3/8 ♪ ♪ ♪	4/8 ♪ ♪ ♪ ♪

89. A group of three notes is occasionally used in simple time to fill a beat, in which case the time signature is not changed but the notes are grouped in threes with a figure three against them. This group is known as a TRIPLET:

Obviously if the beats in a piece of music are consistently divided into threes, it is more convenient to use a compound time signature than to label each group as a triplet. (See para. 119.)

SCALES

90. In considering scales in chapter I we began with C Major as this is the scale with no sharps or flats in the key signature. The key with one sharp in it (G Major) lies on the note a fifth above C and so the key with two sharps (D Major) lies a fifth above G—and so on. Similarly the key a fifth below C (F Major) has one flat and the key a fifth below that (B♭) has two flats.

91. Continuing thus, we find that

the key a fifth above D has three sharps — A major

92. The key signatures of all the major keys so far are:

C major · G major · D major · A major
no signature · 1 sharp · 2 sharps · 3 sharps

C major · F major · B flat major
no signature · 1 flat · 2 flats

93. The top tetrachord of G major becomes the lower tetrachord of D major, and a sharp has to be written before the C to preserve the shape of the scale of D. This too is indicated in the key signature when D is the key note:

94. Similarly, a sharp before G will indicate that the key note is A.

95. The final sharp in a major key signature is always the seventh note of the scale.

96. If the bass clef is used, key signatures are written thus:

97. Notice that A flat and G sharp are the same notes on the keyboard.

98. Here is the complete range of all the major scales so far with the semitones marked with a slur:

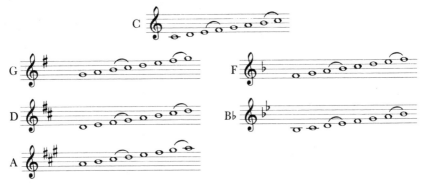

99. Here is the range of minor scales up to three sharps and two flats with their appropriate key signatures. Notice that the seventh degree is chromatically altered in the harmonic minor scale.

A MINOR, RELATIVE TO C MAJOR—"HARMONIC FORM"

MINOR SCALES WITH SHARPS—"HARMONIC FORM"

E minor, relative to G major.

B minor, relative to D major.

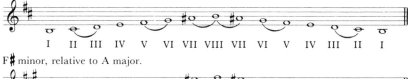

F♯ minor, relative to A major.

MINOR SCALES WITH FLATS—"HARMONIC FORM"

D minor, relative to F major.

G minor, relative to B♭ major.

INTERVALS

100.   Here is the complete list of intervals above the key note of both major and harmonic minor scales:

C Major

Major 2nd	Major 3rd	Perfect 4th	Perfect 5th	Major 6th	Major 7th	Perfect 8ve

A Minor

Major 2nd	Minor 3rd	Perfect 4th	Perfect 5th	Minor 6th	Major 7th	Perfect 8ve

Note that the thirds and sixths are major in major scales and minor in harmonic minor scales. The seventh above the key note requires sharpening in the latter in order to form a true leading note.

101.   Note that the minor sixth contains eight semitones.
   The major sixth contains nine semitones.
   The minor seventh contains ten semitones.
   The major seventh contains eleven semitones.
   The perfect octave contains twelve semitones.
The others are given in para. 61.

102. The fourth degree of the scale is known as the subdominant, and is best thought of as being the note a fifth **below** the Tonic just as the dominant is the fifth **above** the Tonic. Other names are Fah and IV.

TRIADS

103. The triads on I, IV and V are called PRIMARY triads. In a major key they are all major and in a minor key they are minor, the quality of the triad being determined by the quality of the 3rd above the root:

Note that, in a minor key the seventh degree of the scale is the third of the dominant chord which becomes major by reason of the sharpening of the leading note.

104. The triads illustrated in para. 65 are said to be in ROOT POSITION since the root is in the bass. When the root is not in the bass the triad is said to be INVERTED. There are two inverted positions possible for each triad:

The "background" sounds of the three positions of a triad are very similar since they obviously are made up of the same notes and will support the same melody notes, though the individual effects of them vary. Thus:

(a) The root position has a sense of finality and consequently often occurs at cadences and always is used to end a piece.

(b) The 1st inversion has not the same sense of finality and consequently is more useful during a phrase than at the end.

(c) The 2nd inversion has not a sense of finality, but it requires very special treatment if its use is to be convincing; it will be dealt with later.

105.   The root of the chord is indicated by Roman figures which show the step of the scale on which the chord is built. Thus:

In D major, the chord DF♯A is on the Tonic note and is indicated by Ia. The a is generally omitted and taken for granted.

When the chord is in first inversion, it is indicated by Ib.

When it is in second inversion, it is indicated by Ic.

And similarly with all the other triads of a key.

PITCH

106. If it is desired to extend the use of notes outside the range of chapter II, any number of leger lines may be used above or below either stave. It is entirely a matter of convenience.

107. Here is the scale of G above the treble stave:

and below the bass stave:

108. Leger lines can be confusing so the notes are occasionally written an octave above or below their pitch and the displacement is indicated by an *8* and a dotted line below or above them showing that they are to be transposed by an octave.

Thus  becomes

simpler to read when written:

In some music the figure *8* is replaced by *8va*, which has the same effect.

109. In each key, the key note is called Doh and the Tonic; thus it will be seen that the actual notes to which these names apply vary with the scale and key in question.

The same is true of all the other note names.

110. The other notes of the scale are named thus:

The note above the Tonic is known as the supertonic, Ray or II.

The note a third above the Tonic is known as the Mediant, Me or III. The reason is that it is halfway between the Tonic and the Dominant. Similarly the note a third below the Tonic is known as the Submediant, it being halfway between the Tonic and the Subdominant, thinking of the latter as a fifth below the Tonic. The seventh note of the scale is known as the Leading note, Te or VII.

111. Here is the complete table of the names of notes, referring to them in C major and A minor:

Note in C major		A minor		Other names		
C - I	—	A	—	Doh	—	Tonic
D - II	—	B	—	Ray	—	Supertonic
E - III	—	C	—	Me	—	Mediant
F - IV	—	D	—	Fah	—	Subdominant
G - V	—	E	—	Soh	—	Dominant
A - VI	—	F	—	Lah	—	Submediant
B - VII	—	G♯	—	Te	—	Leading note
C - I	—	A	—	Doh	—	Tonic

SCALES

112. In considering scales so far, we began with C major and A minor as these keys have no sharps or flats in the key signatures. We found that G major and E minor had one sharp, D major and B minor had two and A major and F sharp minor had three; also that F major and D minor had one flat while B♭ major and G minor had two flats.

113. Continuing thus, we find that

the key a fifth above A major has four sharps	E major
and the key a fifth above F sharp minor has also four sharps	C sharp minor

The key a fifth below B flat major has three flats	E flat major
the key a fifth below E flat major has four flats	A flat major

and

the key a fifth below G minor has three flats	C minor
the key a fifth below C minor has four flats	F minor

114. It is worth noting that in major keys, the final sharp in the key signature is the leading note of the key, while the final flat in the key signature is the fourth degree of that scale. In minor keys, the final sharp is the supertonic while the final flat is the sixth degree of the scale.

115. We can now extend our range of scales to include these:

Majors:

Harmonic Minors:

C♯ minor, relative to E major.

C minor, relative to E♭ major.

F minor, relative to A♭ major.

116. The large step from the sixth degree to the seventh in the harmonic minor scale makes this awkward to sing in tune. And so, in the rising scale, the sixth note may be sharpened as well as the seventh. Descending, this sounds awkward and so both sixth and seventh degrees are naturalised or flattened. This is known as the MELODIC form, since it is smoother and less angular than the harmonic form.

117. Here is the range of Melodic minor scales:

MINOR SCALES WITH SHARPS—"MELODIC FORM"

A minor, relative to C major

E minor, relative to G major.

B minor, relative to D major.

F♯ minor, relative to A major.

C♯ minor, relative to E major.

MINOR SCALES WITH FLATS—"MELODIC FORM"

D minor, relative to F major.

G minor, relative to B♭ major.

C minor, relative to E♭ major.

F minor, relative to A♭ major.

TO REWRITE A PIECE OF MUSIC IN A DIFFERENT CLEF

118. It is often necessary to transpose a melody an octave from bass to treble clef or vice-versa. If the position of the notes on the stave is known thoroughly there should be no difficulty in this, the only mistake that is often made is transposing the given passage two octaves instead of one. Make sure that when one octave is asked for there is only one octave between the notes:

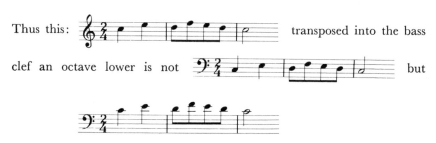

Thus this: ... transposed into the bass clef an octave lower is not ... but

N.B. Once the position of the first note has been determined, try and write, judging by interval from note to note, and try always to hear what you write. You will be less likely to make slips if you can imagine the sound of everything you write.

COMPOUND TIME

119. If these two tunes are examined, it will be found that there are two accented beats in each bar on both:

(a)

(b) etc.

But obviously the basic rhythm is not the same. In (a) the beat divides naturally into two subdivisions whereas in (b) the beat divides into groups of three.

    (a) is in SIMPLE time
    (b) is in COMPOUND time.

Notice that, though in (b) there are six quavers in the bar, there are only two main beats, so that each beat contains three quavers. In compound time the beat always contains groups of three, whether they are quavers, semiquavers or crotchets makes no difference.

120. So we arrive at this rule, that the beats in compound time consist of dotted notes, $\downarrow\cdot$, $\downarrow\cdot$ or $\downarrow\cdot$.

121. In writing in compound time the notes must be grouped so that the beats are clearly indicated as in simple time.

122. The time signatures indicate compound time clearly. If the upper figure is a multiple of three, the time is compound.

Thus $\frac{6}{8}$ indicates compound time since the upper figure is divisible by three, and there are two dotted crotchet beats each consisting of three quavers, as in the example in para. 119.

123. A total of six quavers is also present in a bar of $\frac{3}{4}$ but notice the position of the accents:

Compare this with the same notes in $\frac{6}{8}$:

124. From the grouping of the notes and rests within the bar we can find the time signature, remembering especially that notes in different groups must belong to different beats. For example:

There are 6 quavers in the bar, so the time signature might be either $\frac{3}{4}$ or $\frac{6}{8}$. $\frac{3}{4}$ would need to show three crotchet beats, the quavers belonging to individual beats being joined. But the two quavers in the middle of the bar (which would form the second crotchet beat) are *not* joined, so they must belong to different beats, and the signature must be $\frac{6}{8}$:

If the signature were intended to be $\frac{3}{4}$ the two quavers just mentioned would be joined thus:

The same principles must be applied when sounds lasting more than one beat occur:

Here there are 12 semiquavers in the bar, so the possible time signatures are $\frac{3}{4}$, $\frac{6}{8}$, and $\frac{12}{16}$. We can see that $\frac{3}{4}$ is not possible, since the first sound (quaver tied to dotted crotchet) would last *two whole beats*, and would therefore need to be written as a two-beat note—a minim. In $\frac{6}{8}$ the dotted crotchet at the beginning of the bar would represent one beat, and in $\frac{12}{16}$ two beats, so either might be correct. In the second half of the bar, however, we note that the quaver is separated from the group of three semiquavers, so they must belong to two different beats. The signature must therefore be $\frac{12}{16}$. If the bar were to be written in $\frac{6}{8}$ it would have to appear thus:

The use of the rest between notes on the same tail is quite correct, provided that all the notes belong to the *same beat*.

125. This table gives the different time signatures and shows the corresponding simple and compound times:

	DUPLE		TRIPLE		QUADRUPLE	
SIMPLE	𝄴 or $\frac{2}{2}$ 𝅗𝅥 𝅗𝅥		$\frac{3}{2}$ 𝅗𝅥 𝅗𝅥 𝅗𝅥		𝄴 or $\frac{4}{2}$ 𝅗𝅥 𝅗𝅥 𝅗𝅥 𝅗𝅥	
	$\frac{2}{4}$ ♩ ♩		$\frac{3}{4}$ ♩ ♩ ♩		C or $\frac{4}{4}$ ♩ ♩ ♩ ♩	
	$\frac{2}{8}$ ♪ ♪		$\frac{3}{8}$ ♪ ♪ ♪		$\frac{4}{8}$ ♪ ♪ ♪ ♪	
COMPOUND	$\frac{6}{4}$ 𝅗𝅥. 𝅗𝅥.		$\frac{9}{4}$ 𝅗𝅥. 𝅗𝅥. 𝅗𝅥.		$\frac{12}{4}$ 𝅗𝅥. 𝅗𝅥. 𝅗𝅥. 𝅗𝅥.	
	$\frac{6}{8}$ ♩. ♩.		$\frac{9}{8}$ ♩. ♩. ♩.		$\frac{12}{8}$ ♩. ♩. ♩. ♩.	
	$\frac{6}{16}$ ♪. ♪.		$\frac{9}{16}$ ♪. ♪. ♪.		$\frac{12}{16}$ ♪. ♪. ♪. ♪.	

If the top figure of a simple time is multiplied by three and the bottom one by two, the corresponding compound time signature is ascertained.

TIME

126. Barring, too, should present few problems not already dealt with. Notice that when a phrase begins with an odd note or group of notes not adding up to a complete bar, like:

the last bar of all will almost certainly be incomplete, and the incomplete first bar and the incomplete last bar should add up to a complete bar.

A group of notes at the beginning, before the first strong accent, is known as an ANACRUSIS, or a group of UP BEATS.

127. Rests are also grouped to show beats. Each beat must be complete, and each part of a beat must be completed before adding the next part. In this example the first part of the first beat is a quaver, so the crotchet must be completed before dealing with the dot:

Thus— $\begin{smallmatrix}6\\8\end{smallmatrix}$ ♪ 𝄾 𝄾 𝄿· but *not* $\begin{smallmatrix}6\\8\end{smallmatrix}$ ♪ 𝄾 𝄾·

and— $\begin{smallmatrix}6\\8\end{smallmatrix}$ ♪𝄿 𝄾 𝄾 𝄿· but *not* $\begin{smallmatrix}6\\8\end{smallmatrix}$ ♪ 𝄾 𝄿 𝄿·

N.B. If the first and second divisions of any beat in compound time are silent, a rest equal to the sum of the two divisions may be used. If the second and third divisions of any beat in compound time are silent however, two rests must be used of one division or pulse each:

128. To show a single sound with three beats in compound time it is necessary to use two notes, a dotted two-beat note and then, tied to it, a dotted one-beat note:

129. The barring of unbarred sentences in compound time is no more complex than it is in simple time. First note how the grouping of notes takes place, always remembering that the beginning may not be on the first beat of the bar:

Then note the regular recurrence of accents and the position of the cadence in relation to the strong beats:

This example has accents as marked. These are the strong ones, not just the beats.

This too has accents on strong beats as marked.

Now put bar lines before these accents in each of these and it will be clear that the time signatures are $\frac{6}{8}$ and $\frac{9}{8}$ respectively.

Note that not all melodies begin on the first beat of the bar.

130. When completing a bar with rests, remember to complete any un-finished beats before adding the rests to complete the whole bar. The beat grouping of the bar must always be absolutely clear:

and:

131. An accent caused by a long note being displaced on to a weak beat is known as SYNCOPATION. Example:

Rests on the strong beats may also give the impression of a displaced accent and come under the same heading:

Syncopation may also occur in compound time, but the beat positions must always be kept clear:

INTERVALS

132. In considering the intervals formed on the tonic of the minor scale, it will be realised that the unstable nature of the sixth and seventh degrees of the scale affects all the intervals in which they figure. Thus from the tonic to the submediant may be a minor or a major sixth depending on whether the submediant is or is not sharpened.

For example in A minor:
From A to F is a minor sixth
A to F sharp is a major sixth
From A to G is a minor seventh
A to G sharp is a major seventh.

Taking B minor as an example, here are the intervals formed on its tonic note.

	Major 2nd	Minor 3rd	Perfect 4th	Perfect 5th	Minor 6th	Major 6th	Minor 7th	Major 7th	Perfect 8ve
No. of semitones	2	3	5	7	8	9	10	11	12

TRIADS

133. The triads on II, III and VI are known as SECONDARY triads and in a major key they are minor:

II   III   VI

In the harmonic minor keys, II is diminished, III is augmented by reason of the raised leading note, and VI is major.

II   III   VI

Chapter IV

134.   There are often occasions when it is useful to use double flats and double sharps before notes, and these are written ♭♭ and ✗ and lower or raise respectively an already flattened or sharpened note one semitone. Thus:

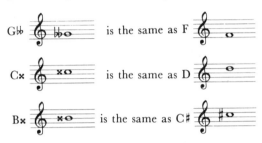

135.   A note with a double sharp before it may be lowered one semitone by placing a single sharp before the note when it appears again in the same bar.
   Similarly to raise a double flattened note one semitone, write a single flat:

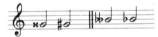

N.B.—This is not a universal practice, and it will be found that in many cases a double sharp or a double flat is first cancelled out by a natural before the single sharp or flat is added:

136.   It is now possible to refer to every note on the piano by several names. Here they are:

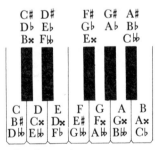

Notice that G sharp—A flat has only two names, all the rest have three.

These names are called ENHARMONIC EQUIVALENTS. Thus G flat is the enharmonic equivalent of F sharp, and the scale of F sharp may be changed enharmonically into G flat—on the piano the notes are identical.

137. Here are the remaining major scales with their semitones marked with slurs and with their key signatures:

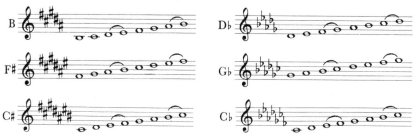

138. Here are the remaining minor scales with their key signatures and with their semitones marked with slurs:

(a) Harmonic minors

G♯ minor, relative to B major.

D♯ minor, relative to F♯ major.

A♯ minor, relative to C♯ major.

B♭ minor, relative to D♭ major.

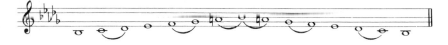

E♭ minor, relative to G♭ major.

Ab minor, relative to Cb major.

(b) Melodic minors

G♯ minor, relative to B major.

D♯ minor, relative to F♯ major.

A♯ minor, relative to C♯ major.

Bb minor, relative to Db major.

Eb minor, relative to Gb major.

Ab minor, relative to Cb major.

Here is the circle of all the keys with the relative minors inside corresponding to their relative majors:

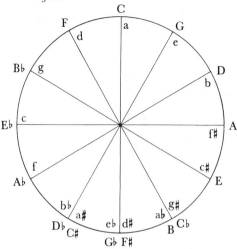

TRANSPOSITION

139. Transposition has already been dealt with to some extent. Even when both the key and the clef change, there should be no difficulty provided that the following steps are carried out:

(a) Find the key of the given melody.

(b) Insert the key signature of the new key and the time signature.

(c) Find the degree of the scale that the melody starts on.

(d) Put the same length of note on the corresponding degree of the new key.

(e) Using the same note values, grouping, barring, etc., as in the original melody, write the notes in the new key, proceeding from one to the next by recognition of the intervals between them. Try and hear the melody as you write.

(f) See that accidentals are inserted, remembering that a raised note in the original melody must be raised in the transposed melody and a lowered one in the original melody lowered in the transposed one.

(g) Remember that a sharp in the original melody may become a natural in the transposed one and similarly a natural may become a flat, and vice versa in both cases. For example:

transposed up an augmented second becomes:

32

Notice how the B natural and E natural of the original become C double sharp and F double sharp when transposed, and how the A natural becomes a B sharp. Another example:

transposed up a minor third and into the treble clef becomes:

140. It is possible, without altering the pitch of the actual notes, to rewrite a passage in, for example, D flat major in C sharp major. This is called rewriting in the ENHARMONIC EQUIVALENT. Example: This,

rewritten a minor third higher is:

Notice the number of flats in the key signature and the unnecessary complexity of double flats as accidentals.
Rewritten in the enharmonic equivalent, it becomes much clearer:

TO FIND THE KEY OF A GIVEN MELODY

141. Deciding on the key of a melody is straightforward so long as certain things are kept in view. Once the key has been found, it will be a simple matter to supply the key signature. Always see that the order of sharps and flats is correct.

142. Not all melodies end on the tonic. To discover the key of a melody in the major which has sharps in it, find out which is the last one present from the order of key signature sharps. This will be the leading note of the key and the key will be the one that lies a semitone above it. This is the order of sharps up to six:

But try above all to feel the 'home' quality of the key note. In the following example the sharps are F sharp, C sharp, G sharp and D sharp. D sharp is the last in the key signature order, and so the key note lies a semitone above the D sharp. Therefore the key is E major and the key signature of four sharps may be put in the space after the clef:

143. Similarly if the melody in the major has flats in it, the last flat present in the order of key signature is the fourth note of the scale. The order of flats is:

The following example has B flat, E flat, A flat, D flat and G flat. G flat is the last one in the order and so our key note is D flat:

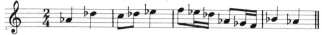

144. To find the key of a piece in the minor, look for the last sharp in the key signature order if it has sharps. This will be the leading note as before. If there is a double sharp in the piece it will almost certainly be the leading note. If there are no sharps look for the last flat note in the key signature order; it will be the *sixth* degree of the scale. If it is not certain whether the key is major or minor, it will be necessary to try each and see if one of them fits; but a general rule may be found helpful—if the melody has sharps and all the sharps up to the sharpest note present are not to be found, the key will certainly be minor. Similarly if all the flats in the key signature order are not present up to the flattest note, the key will be minor. One or two examples will make this clear:

(a)

In the above example (a) the sharpest note is E sharp, which is the leading note of F sharp major, but this has only three other sharps, on F, C and G. Both the D and the A sharps are missing. Therefore the key must be F sharp *minor*.

(b)

In example (b) the flattest note in key signature order is D flat which is the fourth degree of A flat major and the sixth degree of its relative minor, F minor. However the E flat which would indicate A flat major is missing and so the key is F minor.

(c)

In example (c) there are both flats and sharps. The F sharp is obviously the sharpest note and is the leading note of G. There are two flats among the other notes which are also present in the key signature of that key and so the key is G minor.

But in all these try to hear the home feeling of the key note.

145. The only difficulty that may be encountered is when there are sharps, flats and naturals mixed:

146. In the above, there are obviously two flats which suggest B flat major or G minor. But there are also present three sharps. Treating each of these as leading notes, the F sharp would suggest G minor, the C sharp D minor and the G sharp A minor. The presence of E flat cancels out D minor and the E flat and B flat cancel out A minor, so that one is left with G minor. If the example is played over, this will feel like the home tonic. Therefore the other sharps are only chromatic decorations.

If one tries to take the three sharps as the key signature, the result bears so little resemblance to either A major or F sharp minor that one must reject it forthwith.

In this example, however, the two flats are not those of a possible key signature and so may be safely treated as chromatic decorations. Only the E and the A are flattened and if they were part of a key signature, the B would have to be flattened too. The sharps are F sharp, C sharp, E sharp and A sharp. But on looking at the key signature order of sharps we find that both the G and the D which one would have expected to be sharpened are natural, so that one of these sharps must be the leading note of what is probably a minor key. The F sharp and the C sharp are the first two sharps in the key signature order so that it may be assumed that they are part of the actual key signature. If the E sharp is taken as the leading note, the key would be F sharp minor and one would expect a G sharp in the melody, which is not present. The A sharp is the leading note of B minor which feels right as the key note, and the E sharp is obviously a chromatic decoration and is in any case cancelled in the next beat. Therefore the key is B minor.

IRREGULAR GROUPING WITHIN THE BEAT

147.   Sometimes notes are irregularly grouped, that is, the beat is divided into an abnormal number of smaller notes. The triplet has already been referred to as an example of this. Other irregular groups are:

A DUPLET occurs only in compound time. It is a group of two notes played in the time of three of the same kind; the dotted beat is for the moment treated as if it were undotted (Ex. (a)).

A QUADRUPLET is a group of four notes played in the time of three (Ex. (b)).

A QUINTUPLET is a group of five notes played in the time of four of the same kind in simple time (Ex. (c)), or of three of the same kind in compound time (Ex. (d)).

A SEXTOLET is a group of six notes played in the time of four of the same kind (Ex. (e)). It is also known as a sextuplet.

A SEPTOLET is a group of seven notes played in the time of four or six of the same kind (Ex. (f) and (g)), also known as septuplet.

148.   The key to all these problems of rhythm is the aural recognition of the relative strengths of the beats and their accents. This can only be learnt by practice in the recognition from examples played or sung, and can never be developed by working them out on paper.

149. Even when the time signature is given in an unbarred sentence, unless the sentence begins on the first beat of the bar, the accents must be felt or it will never be possible to put the bar lines in the right places:

150. It is practically impossible to distinguish $\frac{6}{8}$ from $\frac{12}{8}$ unless beat one in the latter has an exaggerated accent.

Even then the grouping of bars in $\frac{6}{8}$ in twos will render the difference un-detectable. In the following examples is (a) more correct than (b)?

It is doubtful. No musician will accent the first quaver of the second bar of the example in $\frac{6}{8}$ as strongly as the first quaver of the first bar.

INTERVALS

151. We must now deal with the intervals on all degrees of the scales, major and minor, both forms.

We will take the Major Scale first.

152. Fourths and Fifths are known as PERFECT intervals, but there are AUGMENTED FOURTHS and DIMINISHED FIFTHS in the notes of the major scale.

A perfect fourth contains 5 semitones

An augmented fourth contains 6 semitones

A perfect fifth contains 7 semitones

A diminished fifth contains 6 semitones.

Thus the sound of the augmented fourth and the diminished fifth are identical, at least on the piano.

153. All the fifths on the notes of the major scale are perfect except that on the leading note (the seventh degree), which is diminished and contains six semitones.

154. All the fourths are perfect except that on the subdominant (the fourth degree) which is augmented and contains six semitones.

155. The thirds on the tonic, subdominant and dominant are major and contain four semitones.

All the others on the supertonic, mediant, submediant and leading note are minor and contain three semitones:

156. The sixths on the tonic, supertonic, subdominant and dominant are major and contain nine semitones.

The sixths on the other notes, mediant, submediant and leading note are minor and contain eight semitones:

157. The seconds, with the exceptions of those on the mediant and the leading note which are semitones and therefore minor, are all major and contain two semitones. Minor seconds contain one semitone.

158. All the sevenths are minor except those on the tonic and the subdominant. A minor seventh contains ten semitones and the sevenths on the tonic and subdominant contain eleven semitones:

159. Intervals in the Minor Scale.

The variable nature of the sixth and seventh degrees make these intervals more complex than they are in the major scale, and augmented and diminished fourths and fifths, augmented seconds and diminished sevenths are to be found.

160. It should be noted that only perfect and major intervals can be augmented, while only perfect and minor intervals can be diminished.

161. A major interval may be made minor by raising its lower note or by lowering its upper note a chromatic semitone:

162. A minor interval may be made major by lowering its lower note or by raising its upper note a chromatic semitone:

163. A perfect interval may be made augmented or diminished by chromatic alteration of one of its notes in the same way:

164. A major interval may be made augmented and a minor one diminished by chromatically altering one of its notes:

165. If the two notes forming an interval are both found among the notes of the scale of any one key, the interval is said to be diatonic in that key:

both in D♭ major

If they are not to be so found then the interval is said to be chromatic:

166. If asked to find the name of an interval, remember that from a tonic of a major key the second, third, sixth and seventh are all major, the fourth and fifth being perfect. Therefore take the lower note of the interval and imagine it as the key note, doh. If the upper note is part of the major scale on the lower note, then it will be one of the above intervals. If it does not fit into the notes of the scale, count the numerical value of the interval and find out whether the upper note is higher or lower than the corresponding one in the major scale.

Thus   is a major sixth in C major and contains nine semitones.

But   contains eight semitones and so is a minor sixth.

167. A study of the scale of C minor and the following table should make the intervals of the minor scale clear.

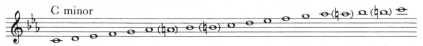

168.   This table gives all the intervals in the minor scales.

	Tonic	Super tonic	Mediant	Subdominant	Dominant	Submediant	Leading note	Tonic
Tonic	Octave	Major 2	Minor 3	Perfect 4	Perfect 5	Minor or Major 6	Minor or Major 7	8
Super tonic	Minor 7	Octave	Minor 2	Minor 3	Perfect 4	Diminished or Perfect 5	Minor or Major 6	Minor 7
Mediant	Major 6	Major 7	Octave	Major 2	Major 3	Perfect or Augmented 4	Perfect or Augmented 5	Major 6
Subdominant	Perfect 5	Major 6	Minor 7	Octave	Major 2	Minor or Major 3	Perfect or Augmented 4	Perfect 5
Dominant	Perfect 4	Perfect 5	Minor 6	Minor 7	Octave	Minor or Major 2	Minor or Major 3	Perfect 4
Submediant	Major or Minor 3	Augmented or Perfect 4	Perfect or Diminished 5	Major or Minor 6	Major or Minor 7	Octave	Major, Minor, or Augmented 2	Major or Minor 3
Leading note	Major or Minor 2	Major or Minor 3	Perfect or Diminished 4	Perfect or Diminished 5	Major or Minor 6	Major, Minor, or Diminished 7	Octave	Major or Minor 2

169.   Seconds.   Those on the tonic, mediant and subdominant are major.
That on the supertonic is minor.
Those on the dominant and leading note may be minor or major.
That on the submediant may be minor, major or augmented.

Major   Minor   Major   Major   Major   Minor   Maj. Aug.   Min.   Maj.   Maj. Min.

170.   Thirds.   Those on the tonic and supertonic are minor.
That on the mediant is major.
Those on the subdominant, dominant, submediant and leading note may be major or minor.

Min.   Min.   Maj.   Min. Maj.   Min. Maj.   Maj. Min.   Maj. Min.

171.   Fourths.   Those on the tonic, supertonic and dominant are perfect.
Those on the mediant, subdominant and submediant may be perfect or augmented.
That on the leading note may be perfect or diminished.

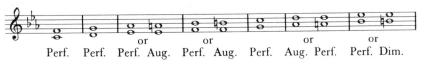

Perf.   Perf.   Perf.   Aug.   Perf.   Aug.   Perf.   Aug.   Perf.   Perf. Dim.

172. Fifths. Those on the tonic, subdominant and dominant are perfect. Those on the supertonic, submediant and leading note may be perfect or diminished.
That on the mediant may be perfect or augmented.

Perf. Dim. Perf.   Perf. Aug.   Perf.   Perf.   Perf. Dim.   Perf. Dim.

173. Sixths. Those on the tonic, supertonic, submediant and leading note may be major or minor.
Those on the mediant and subdominant are major.
That on the dominant is minor.

Min. Maj. Min. Maj.   Maj.   Maj.   Min.   Maj. Min.   Maj. Min.

174. Sevenths. Those on the supertonic, subdominant and dominant are minor.
That on the mediant is major.
Those on the tonic and submediant may be major or minor.
That on the leading note may be major, minor or diminished.

or   or   or or or
Min. Maj. Min.   Maj.   Min.   Min.   Maj. Min.   Min. Dim. Maj. Min.

175. It is now necessary to consider the inversion of intervals. If the lower note of an interval is transposed up an octave or if the upper note is transposed down an octave, the interval is said to be INVERTED. Thus:

becomes   or

176. The following should be memorised:
(a) A perfect interval inverted remains perfect
    A major interval inverted becomes minor
    A minor interval inverted becomes major
    A diminished interval inverted becomes augmented
    An augmented interval inverted becomes diminished
(b) A second inverted becomes a seventh
    A third inverted becomes a sixth
    A fourth inverted becomes a fifth
    A fifth inverted becomes a fourth
    A sixth inverted becomes a third
    A seventh inverted becomes a second.

Examples:

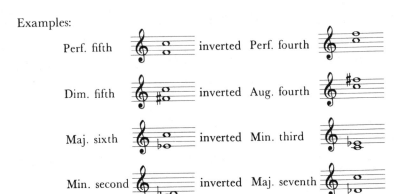

Perf. fifth — inverted Perf. fourth

Dim. fifth — inverted Aug. fourth

Maj. sixth — inverted Min. third

Min. second — inverted Maj. seventh

TRIADS

177. A clearer sense of tonality is maintained if chords are built from the notes of the harmonic minor scale; as an example, here are the triads of the key of C minor, so derived.

I   II   III   IV   V   VI   VII

Chords involving the raised 6th and the lowered 7th require care in use if they are not to undermine the sense of key.

178. These triads are subject to inversion in the same way as the primary triads described in paras. 103 and 104. Triad positions are indicated as in para. 104.

179. One further triad remains to be identified, namely, that on the Leading note, VII. In a major key it is a diminished triad, the interval between its root and fifth being a diminished fifth.

In a minor key, it is a diminished triad also except when the descending form of the melodic minor scale is being used. Examples are:

D Major   D Minor   and

VII

180. It is worth remembering here that certain chords may vary in their qualities when they are used in minor keys, by reason of the variability of the sixth and seventh degrees of the scale in the melodic minor. These are:

II may be diminished or minor.
III may be major or augmented.
VI may be major or diminished.
VII may be diminished or major.

Examples:

C minor II

Diminished Minor

C minor III

Augmented Major

C minor VI

Major Diminished

C minor VII

Diminished Major

ORNAMENTS and ABBREVIATIONS

181. *The Acciaccatura*

Written as a small note with a stroke through its tail.

Played on the beat as quickly as convenient, normally about a demi-semiquaver in length:

182. *The Appoggiatura*

Written as a small note without a line through its tail.

It receives half the value of the note it precedes:

If it is placed before a dotted note it receives two thirds of its value:

42

If the dotted note divides normally into two equal halves, the appoggiatura receives half the value of the note:

Similarly if two notes are tied together in compound time, the first taking the space of a beat and the second taking less, the appoggiatura receives the value of the whole of the beat:

183. *The Upper Mordent or Pralltriller*

Written (∿) above or below the note to which it applies.

Played as fast as is convenient consistent with the speed and style of the music, but always on the beat:

An accidental above the sign affects the auxiliary note:

184. *The Lower Mordent* is like the pralltriller but the auxiliary note is below the principal note. The sign is as for the pralltriller but with a line vertically through it (∿):

Chapter V

ORNAMENTS AND ABBREVIATIONS

185. *The Turn*

Written (∾) above the note.

Consists of the upper auxiliary note followed by the principal note followed by the lower auxiliary note followed by the principal note:

The turn commences on the beat and with the upper note.

If the turn is on a note that occurs after a rest, it must commence with the principal note and will become a quintuplet:

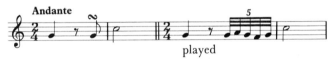

Note also that an accidental below the sign affects the lower note of the turn, and one above it affects the upper note:

Notice in this last example that the E flat must be cancelled for the quaver E natural.

186 *The Inverted Turn* is like the turn but with a vertical line through it, (⌀). It is also sometimes written thus (𝟤).

The inverted turn commences on the beat with the lower auxiliary first:

Both the turn and the inverted turn may be written after the principal note, specially if the principal note is a long one, when the turn will be played as late as is conveniently possible:

Observe, however, the note lengths in allegro and also the accidental below the sign.

If the turn is written after a dotted note that involves a fraction of a beat, the turn becomes a triplet occupying the second third of the dotted principal note:

187. *The Arpeggio*

Written as a wavy line before a chord.

Played as a rapid arpeggio commencing on the beat with the lowest note:

Note that the notes are tied into the chord.

The Arpeggio chord may be combined with the Appoggiatura and the Acciaccatura in which case the note to which the appoggiatura or the acciaccatura applies is indicated by a short slur:

Similarly the Appoggiatura and the Acciaccatura may each be applied to any note of a chord without arpeggio:

188. *The Trill or Shake*

Written (*tr*⌁) and sometimes (*tr*).

It consists of a rapid alternation of the principal note with the note above it. It is normal to write trills in demisemiquavers up to allegro but it is seldom desirable to play them so strictly.

The trill commences on the principal note in the music of the nineteenth century, but up to and including Mozart and Haydn it is normal to commence on the note above the principal note. The trill will commence on the note above the principal in all periods if

(a) it is preceded by its principal note
(b) it is preceded by an acciaccatura.

It is normal practice to end a trill with a turn, whether such is indicated or not, unless the trill is so short as to render a turn undesirable:

Sometimes the turn at the end is indicated in small notes, and these are taken at the same speed as the trill, but if the rhythm of the final notes is indicated in full-sized notes they take their written value:

A trill on a very short note is played like a turn on that note. Whether it commences on the principal note or on the note above depends on the various factors already mentioned:

If the trill is preceded by small notes, these are incorporated into the trill:

played

A trill on a dotted note that involves a fraction of a beat will stop on the dot. A turn may or may not be added according to taste:

played

A trill on a dotted note which is a beat in compound time must be treated in the same way as a trill on an undotted note, and the trill must go on to the end of the dotted note:

played

In a minor key, if the trill is on the leading note, remember to avoid the augmented second in the turn by raising the sixth degree even when it is not indicated in the sign:

played

Note that all these ornaments are affected in a similar way by accidentals, and the note lengths of all of them will vary with the speed of the music.

189. These signs indicate repetition of a beat, a bar or a section of a bar, **/ , ⅞ , //** :

The rapid repetition of a note is indicated thus (note that the number of strokes through the tail of the note indicates the speed of the vibration):

The tremolo between two notes is written thus (note again the relationship of the number of strokes through the tail to the rate of vibration):

Old signs for trills starting with turns and inverted turns, also finishing with turns and inverted turns are as follows:

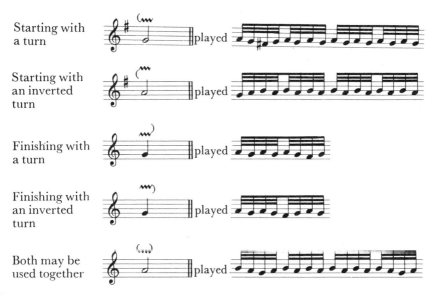

This generally indicates a trill preceded by an appoggiatura:

ALTO AND TENOR CLEFS

190. In addition to the G and F clefs there are two others in common use today. These are the Alto and Tenor clefs, also known as C clefs since they mark on the stave the position of middle C. They are useful because they reduce the need for leger lines. A C clef may be put on any line of the stave and is commonly found thus in music up to the middle of the eighteenth century.

191. The ALTO CLEF   Middle C   covers approximately the compass of the alto voice.

It is used when writing for the viola. Notice that the interval of a 5th separates middle C from the outside lines of the stave in each direction.

The notes on the alto clef, with the same notes on the F and G clefs for comparison, are:

Note the position of the sharps and flats in the key signatures:

192. The TENOR CLEF   Middle C   similarly covers approximately the range of the tenor voice.

It is also used in writing for the 'cello, the bassoon and the trombone. The notes in the tenor clef are:

Again note the position of the sharps and flats in the key signatures:

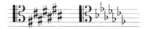

193. A piece of 4-part writing written on two staves may be rewritten in "OPEN SCORE" as for four voices and using C clefs for alto and tenor parts, each part having its own stave:

The same passage in Open Vocal Score:

Treble

Alto

Tenor

Bass

Observe carefully the notes affected by accidentals. In close score, an accidental used to inflect a note in one part may also inflect a note in another part without its being rewritten. In rewriting in open score, the accidental must be applied to the relevant note in both affected parts. Another example will make this clear:

In open score the lower part in this example must be rewritten with the E natural and F sharp added in the 1st bar. In the 2nd bar, the A flat only affects the lower part and so in open score the upper part does not need the natural before the A. Here it is rewritten:

194. Here is the first example in the previous paragraph rewritten for string quartet; in this case remember that the two upper parts are written for two violins using the G Clef, the third part is written for viola in the alto clef and the bass is written for 'cello in the F clef or possibly the tenor clef if the notes are exceptionally high:

195. To rewrite a piece of music in short score on two staves from a piece in open score is simple. See that the stems of the treble and tenor parts go upwards and those of the alto and bass downwards. Then check over all the accidentals and see that there are none that are redundant.

PHRASING

196. Music is divided into sentences and phrases just as prose and poetry are.

197. A simple sentence frequently consists of two phrases known as FORE-PHRASE and AFTER-PHRASE, or often as STATEMENT and RESPONSE:

198. Note that in the second of these the phrases commence squarely on the first beats of the bars, but in the first they do not. If the first phrase commences with an up-beat or anacrusis, it is most likely that each of the other phrases will do the same.

199. A phrase is closed by a CADENCE. Some cadences are more final than others, the most final in effect occurring at the end of the sentence, like the full stop in prose.

200. Frequently however a sentence contains more than two phrases. This one has three:

Mozart: *Sonata, K. 332*

201. Phrases are not always the same length. Shorter phrases in a sentence are often associated with repetition or sequence. In this one the short third phrase is repeated:

Mozart: *Symphony, K. 551*

202. A sequence is merely a repeat of a phrase at a different pitch.

203. The length of phrases can generally be felt by playing them or by singing them. A phrase is marked by a slur from its first note to its last, but note that composers use the slur to mark the bowing for string instruments and for detail of articulation and generally leave the phrase lengths to the common sense and musicianship of the player. If the actual phrase lengths are to be marked, it is a good plan to use square brackets, thus: ⌐￣￣￣⌐ . In marking the phrases of a melody notice should be taken of:

    (a) natural cadence points
    (b) repeated rhythmic fragments

(c) the presence or absence of anacrusis. This takes place when a phrase begins with an unaccented note, or notes—an upbeat, as in this example.

Sequential repetitions even if they are inexact, as below, should be marked with a slur separately even though they are very short:

204. Here is an example of phrases three bars long:

205. Some phrases appear to subdivide, and this has led some authorities to call the divisions of phrases "sections"; but the length of phrases really depends on a variety of factors such as speed, degree of finality of endings, relationship to other phrases in the sentence of which it is a part, so that it is simplest to refer to all subdivisions of sentences as phrases. The use of terms like "figure" or "motif" is not really accurate in describing a subdivision of a phrase since both of these refer more to groups of notes displaying some characteristic feature of rhythm or melodic outline which has further significance. In a sonata by Mozart or Beethoven, the vitality and sense of movement of the music depends upon, among other things, variety in the lengths of phrases, and even songs like those of Schubert may show a considerable variety in length of phrase: "Danksagung an den Bach" from "Die schöne Müllerin" is a good example. Here is a remarkably freely phrased melody from Mozart's opera "Don Giovanni":

206. Phrases may be extended by avoidance of a cadence or by sequential extension, or they may naturally fall into shapes outside the normal expected ones like this rambling second theme of Dvorak's *D minor Symphony*:

It is impossible and it would be unmusical to lay down rules about how long a phrase should be.

207. A melody may be said to have balance when its various phrases form a satisfactory whole. Generally a melody reaches a central point and what follows corresponds to, or complements, what comes first, but it is not necessary for the second half of a melody in two sections to follow the exact rhythmic pattern of the first. The example in para. 201 above demonstrates this point.

208. For the sake of simplicity, we will examine a melody which divides naturally into two parts. The actual phrases are of two-bar length as dictated by the lines of the text, so that the melody really has four two-bar phrases.

There is an obvious feeling of incompleteness at the end of the second phrase, but the two parts of the melody are similar in length and in rhythmic structure, and there is a finality about the end that makes it satisfactorily complete. Note how the second phrase rises to a climax which really comes at the beginning of the third phrase. Thereafter there is a falling off to the end, though the last phrase does rise to the tonic. This is a particularly fine example of a balanced melody.

209. When completing a sentence by adding an after-phrase, these points should be borne in mind, but remember, too, that variety is always desirable.

The main points to watch are:

(a) The cadence endings of the two phrases should not be the same.

(b) An upward movement in one phrase may well be complemented by a falling one in the other, and vice versa.

(c) There should be some rhythmic connection between the two, though exactly parallel-rhythmic structure is undesirable.

(d) The after-phrase may usefully employ one or more of the rhythmic features of the fore-phrase.

(e) The after-phrase should end in the tonic key.

(f) It is often desirable to have a climax during the after-phrase.

(g) Try to make use of any particularly conspicuous figure of the fore-phrase in the after-phrase.

It is impossible to lay down any laws about this type of problem; each example must be considered on its own merits and on its own grounds. The aim must be to write a sentence that is coherent and consistent in its own terms.

210. Not all melodies change their key; modulating melodies will be dealt with later (see chap. VI).

211. Generally speaking, if a melody is in two parts, the second half will be at least as long, if not longer than the first. It is very difficult to balance a phrase of four bars with one of three, though the reverse is common, that is, a three bar phrase followed by one of four.

212. If the melody in para. 208 is examined, it will be seen that it falls into two clear sections marked in the example by square brackets. The first four bar phrase is called the "forephrase" and the second four bars the "after-phrase". Each of these phrases ends with a cadence (see para. 215 ff). The first phrase ends with an imperfect cadence while the second ends with a form of a final cadence, in this case it is not quite a perfect one since the melody has modal features that are outside the normal language of Bach or Handel.

In writing afterphrases to a given opening phrase, it is necessary to consider the length of the given phrase, the cadences and the general shape and balance of one phrase against the other. The rise and fall in pitch should be complementary in the two phrases.

CHORDS

213. A more accurate and musical way of labelling chords with figures is the old method used by Bach and Handel and the other composers of the Baroque period (approximately 1600 until 1760), the so-called "figured bass". The figures do NOT refer to the roots of the chords but relate the chord position to the note in the bass.

The position of the chord above the BASS note is indicated by figures written underneath which refer to the intervals between the bass notes and the upper notes:

5	6	6
3	3	4
root position	1st inversion	2nd inversion

When this system is in use, the figures $\frac{5}{3}$ are generally omitted and it is assumed that any bass note with no figures under it bears a chord in root position above it. Further, the $\frac{6}{3}$ is generally indicated by merely 6, as it is assumed that there will be a 3rd present unless specially shown. The $\frac{6}{4}$ is written in full:

$$\left(\begin{matrix}5\\3\end{matrix}\right) \quad \begin{matrix}6\\(3)\end{matrix} \quad \begin{matrix}6\\4\end{matrix}$$

When several bass notes occur without a change of harmony, a horizontal line below them is used; note the combination of this with other figures.

(a) means that the $\frac{5}{3}$ on C is held as long as the line lasts.

(b) means exactly the same thing. *It is not a continuation of the 6th on E,* since there is a space between the figure 6 and the line.

(c) means the same as (a) or (b). It does not mean a $\frac{5}{3}$ on the second E, which would be written if the line were not there. It therefore means a continuation of the preceding chord.

(d) means that the chord struck at the beginning of the line is held to its end. Observe that the line begins *close to the right side of the figure 6.*

(e) means that B, the 6th of the bass-note D, is continued when G, the 4th of the bass, is added.

(f) means that the chord struck on the first beat is held through the bar.

When an accidental is needed, it is written on the left side of the figure affected, thus: ♮6   ♯6   ♭3

An accidental alone affects the 3rd above the bass note. Examples:

A figure with a stroke through it implies that that note is raised a semitone:

T.S. (tasto solo or played alone) under a bass note indicates that no harmony is to be put above it.

CADENCES

214. The most important notes of a melody to harmonise are those that close the phrases and sentences. These are known as CADENCES.

FORE-PHRASE — Old Song: *Oh, my love's like the red, red rose*

Half Cadence
Chords I to V

AFTER-PHRASE

Full Cadence
Chords V to I

215. There are four principal cadences:
Perfect
Plagal
Imperfect
Interrupted

216. A PERFECT cadence consists of the chord on the dominant followed by the chord on the tonic—V-I. This has a very strong feeling of finality and generally ends a sentence:

and

C: V I V I   C mi: I V I

217. The IMPERFECT cadence or HALF-CLOSE, as its name suggests, has not the finality of the perfect or plagal cadences; it consists of one of several chords followed by the dominant, and ends phrases as a comma does:

I V VI V VI V

I V II V VI V

Ib   V   IIb   V   Ic   V

218. The progression IV-V is known as a MIXED cadence. It is only another name for one form of an imperfect cadence:

and

C: IV   V   IV   V   C mi: IV   V   IV   V

219. The progression IVb-V in a minor key is known as a PHRYGIAN cadence:

Handel: *Largo of 12th Violin Sonata*

example

C: IVb   V   C#mi: V   VI   IVb   V

220. The INTERRUPTED cadence is so called because it starts as if it would be a perfect cadence with the dominant chord but follows it with the sub-mediant; it is, like the imperfect cadence, used as an ending to a phrase but not to a sentence:

and

C: V   VI   V⁷   VI .   C: V⁷   VI   V   VI

Note that the dominant chord in the interrupted cadence may be a dominant seventh.

221. The effect of finality of the perfect cadence may be considerably undermined by using inverted positions for one or both of the chords:

VIIb   I   VIIb   Ib   Vb   I   V   Ib

in which case the cadence is known as an INVERTED PERFECT CADENCE.

222. The PLAGAL cadence is no less final in its effect and consists of the chord on the subdominant followed by that on the tonic. These are the pair of chords to which the "Amen" at the end of hymns is generally sung:

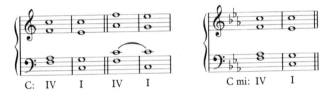

C: IV   I   IV   I   C mi: IV   I

Note that in a perfect or plagal cadence in a minor key, the 3rd of the tonic chord is often made major. This is known as a "Tierce de Picardie":

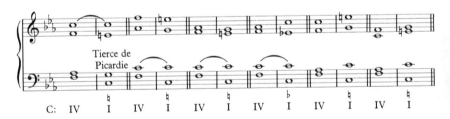

Tierce de Picardie

C: IV   I   IV   I   IV   I   IV   I   IV   I   IV   I

223. The inverted cadence may be used freely in the course of a melody and at phrase ends, but it is unsatisfactory at the end of a sentence.

All cadences may be used inverted and the effects of all possible positions of the chords should be studied by experiment and listening.

224. The student should now be able to put cadence chords at appropriate places in melodies and one or two examples may help to make the procedure clear. The ultimate guide as to choice of cadence must always be the ear, trained by experience.

MELODIC DECORATION

225. A PASSING NOTE is a note outside the prevailing harmony which lies off the beat between two harmony notes and joins them by step. In this example the passing notes are marked by a cross ✕:

Passing notes may occur in pairs or in groups:

A passing note may proceed by oblique motion to an octave but care should be taken when allowing it to proceed to a unison—it should not do so from a semitone's distance:

226. An APPOGGIATURA, also known as an ACCENTED PASSING NOTE, is a non-harmony note which occurs on the beat and resolves by step generally downwards, but occasionally upwards. It may be approached by leap:

227. An AUXILIARY NOTE is a non-harmony note which lies between repetitions of a note that is part of the harmony a step above or below it. It occurs off the beat:

228. CHANGING NOTES are two auxiliaries, one above and one below the harmony note, occurring in succession after the principal note and returning to the harmony note:

229. An ECHAPPÉ, literally, escape note, is a move to a note that is not part of the harmony and is not resolved. If such a note resolves by step it is like an appoggiatura off the beat or an auxiliary:

J. S. Bach: *Chorale*

230. If a note of one chord is retained into the sound of another that does not normally contain it, it is known as a SUSPENSION and resolves in the same way as an appoggiatura, that is, by step downwards, or occasionally upwards. It is only effective when it occurs on a strong beat:

J. S. Bach: *Partita in E minor*

an example

231. RETARDATION is the name given to a discord on a beat resolving upwards. It is only a kind of suspension, or appoggiatura:

232. Suspensions may be decorated in their resolution:

233. The suspension should always be equal to or shorter than the note suspended in the previous bar, so far as the style of the eighteenth and nineteenth centuries is concerned. The suspension short to long tends to obliterate the metrical accent:

234. A note of the harmony may be sounded before that harmony is due while the previous chord is still sounding. This is known as an ANTICIPATION:

J. S. Bach: *Gib dich zurfrieden*

HARMONY IN FOUR PARTS

235. Harmony is generally studied in and written for four voices, Soprano, Alto, Tenor and Bass. The application of its principles to instruments is simple and involves really nothing more than extension of pitch range in the individual parts and any special considerations derived from the techniques of the various instruments.

236. The aim of harmonisation must be to achieve the greatest smoothness and euphony in the combination of voices. The following tips may help you to achieve the effects you want to produce.

237. If you listen to a perfect cadence carefully you will hear that the 3rd of the dominant chord, the leading note, has a strong tendency to move up to the tonic. This is, of course, the real significance of its name:

238. Similarly, if you want to achieve the smoothest effect, each note of the first chord should proceed to the nearest possible note of the second. Leaps in a part tend to make the progression jerky, except when they occur in the bass part.

239. Play these cadences and listen to the effect of all the voices going in the same direction:

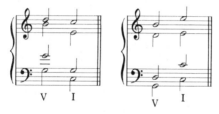

Play these, and see if you do not find them more smooth and satisfactory:

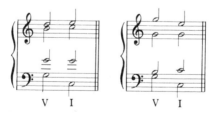

The reason is that some of the parts are moving in contrary motion. This is most noticeable when the bass part moves in contrary motion to the upper parts, and is especially desirable in imperfect and interrupted cadences:

In the progression IV-V, this is more or less obligatory since there is a grave danger of pairs of voices moving in parallel octaves or fifths. This fault is known as consecutives.

240. Consecutive 5ths, and 8ves occur when a pair of voices move from an interval of a 5th apart to another interval of a 5th apart and from an octave or unison apart to another interval of an octave or unison, whether by similar or contrary movement. These examples will make this clear:

This refers to perfect intervals only. A perfect 5th may be followed by a diminished 5th and vice versa without any ill effect.

241. The reason for this is that two different period styles of writing are involved. The earliest melodies in the church were sung in unison or at the octave. At a later period the melodies were doubled in another voice, or voices at the intervals of a 5th and 4th. This was known as "Organum". Still later, movement in 3rds and 6ths was the ideal of euphonious writing. Gradually the independence of the individual parts was achieved, until by Bach's time too many parallel 3rds and 6ths in a row were considered dull and objectionable. What is really happening when parts are allowed to move in consecutive 5ths and octaves is that the stark qualities of an earlier style are being used in a smoother and more expressive later style.

Even momentary bareness caused by the outside parts moving in similar motion to octaves or fifths can sound out of place unless the upper part moves by step. This fault is known as EXPOSED (or HIDDEN) OCTAVES or FIFTHS:

Note these exceptions to this. They sound perfectly smooth and unobtrusive:

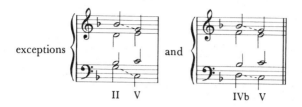

exceptions and

II   V   IVb V

242. When writing 3-note triads for the normal four voices, it is obvious that one of the notes must be doubled:

Doubled Root   Doubled   Doubled
                   Third   Fifth

Normally, it does not matter which note is doubled, but it should be remembered that doubling a note brings it into considerable prominence.

Thus, in a perfect cadence the leading note has such a strong pull to the tonic that, if it is doubled, it will be too prominent and its resolution will sound forced if consecutives are avoided. Therefore do not double the leading note in a perfect cadence.

There is no restriction on doubling the 3rd of other major chords, though if the chords are in first inversion position, such doubling may sound a little awkward unless the voices doubling it move in contrary motion:

II   Ib   IIb

The diminished triad on the leading note of both major and minor scales and that on the supertonic of the minor scale need care. Generally speaking, if you double a note that is discordant with another note, you draw attention to the discord. The root and 5th of a diminished chord are a diminished 5th

apart and are mutually discordant. Therefore the best note to double is
the 3rd from the root. This is especially the case when the chord is in 1st
inversion position, when the 3rd from the root is in the bass:

243. Notice that it is not always possible to have both chords in a perfect
cadence complete without lapsing into consecutives. It is frequently necessary to omit the 5th from one of them:

244. In the interrupted cadence in a minor key, care is necessary to avoid
moving one of the parts by an augmented 2nd. Instead, double the 3rd of
the submediant chord, VI:

245. Augmented intervals in any one part should be avoided for the simple
reason that they are difficult to sing in tune; but diminished intervals may be
used freely provided that the part returns to a note within the leap.

But they are a normal part of instrumental writing.

246. The distribution of the parts and the gaps between the notes of a chord need care. For the most smooth sound the four voices should be spaced fairly evenly with any large gaps between the bass and tenor:

If a treble becomes too separated from the alto, the sound is hollow:

If the lower parts are allowed to descend too far and the tenor to keep too near the bass, the sound is rough and the tenor tends to lose quality of tone:

There should not be more than an octave between any pairs of adjacent voices except the bass and tenor. The effect is lopsided.

247. Double and triple suspensions and appoggiaturas often occur when writing in four parts:

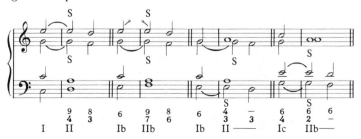

248. In the same way the other unessential notes discussed above may be used in inner parts and so long as they do not create ugly discord they may be used together simultaneously:

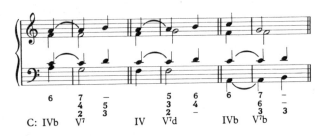

Notice the figuring of these unessential notes.

HARMONISING A MELODY—WRITING A BASS

249. Two things must now be obvious:
(a) an apparently complex and decorated melody may well have a very simple chord background.
(b) the chordal basis will only make sense if the chordal tread moves inevitably and inexorably towards cadence points.

250. When adding chord or harmonic implications to a melody, the simplest possible solution will have the greatest effect in the drive to the cadence.

Many apparently elaborate melodies have a basically simple chordal background like this one from Weber's opera *Der Freischutz:*

This melody contains many notes that are not part of the prevailing harmony

251. It is not desirable to try to imagine a different chord for every note of the melody. If a melody utilises the notes of a chord like this from Haydn's *"Surprise" Symphony:*

it would be foolish to try to harmonise it with a new chord for each note, though it could just be done!

Haydn's own chordal background is much simpler and more musical:

252. Melodies should be thought of in terms of their natural harmonic background, that is the background of chords which will support them satisfactorily. Few melodies need a fresh chord for each note and the aim should always be to use the simplest series of chords that is effective. Even hymn tunes often have several melody notes using the same background chord. Compare:

with:

Schubert: *Heidenröslein*

253. At first glance this would appear to imply a complex chord basis, and it most certainly would if a chord to each note were deemed necessary:

An effective basis is:

254. But a bass line which jumps about from root to root, as in the above example, is dull and characterless, however strong. This bass moves within the same chord basis, but is smoother and more interesting, and the root positions, when they occur, give strength and finality to the whole by shaping the chord tread to the cadences:

255. This bass line may be given interesting decorations by the devices used to decorate a melody, as described above in paras. 225-234.

(1) passing note, (2) and (3) appoggiaturas, (4) auxiliary note, (5) and (6) appoggiaturas, (7) passing note, (8) could be considered a second passing note with (7) or could imply another change of harmony, (9) passing note, (10) a change of harmony beyond that implied in 254 above. It is an excellent feature as it speeds up the rate of chord change and thus makes the cadence more firm.

Note that the essential bass in bar 3 is different from that in para. 253 above, the change being desirable to add interest to the line.

These devices provide the basis of good two-part writing, which should avoid the dullness of a note-against-note texture.

256. ORGAN-POINT, PEDAL-POINT, PEDAL-BASS or PEDAL. These are technical names given to the dominant or the tonic when either is sustained in the bass, whilst harmonies are sounded above it, of which the sustained note does not always form a portion. *A pedal in the bass part*, after the beat on which it is first struck, *does not form the true bass of the harmony*; the part next above the pedal is the *true bass for the time being*.

An INVERTED PEDAL is a tonic or dominant note sustained or repeated in one of the *upper parts*, instead of in the bass.

Other notes may be sustained as pedal notes, but the dominant and the tonic are the most common in use.

WRITING A MELODY ABOVE A BASS

257. When a bass is given, the harmonic background of it can be found in the same way by "feel":

Observe that the notes of the bass are not necessarily the roots of the chords. If this passage were harmonised throughout by root position chords, the succession of sounds would be poor.

258. For harmonising as essential harmonies more notes of the bass than Couperin does, here is a possible chord basis:

and here is a melody above it that fits in with this chord basis:

Notice how much more fussy it is than the original in both harmony and melody.

Chapter VI

MELODY WRITING AND MODULATION

86. So far we have only considered sentences and melodies which do not move into another key. A move into another key is called MODULATION, and is generally made obvious by the appearance of the leading note of the new key:

Bach: Chorale. *Nur mein Jesus ist mein leben.*

260. In a melody a shift of key may be strongly felt without the actual appearance of the new leading note. This is known as IMPLIED MODULATION. (The new leading note will be present in the supporting harmony.)

Bach: *O Jesulein Süss*

261. Melodies in a major key commonly modulate first of all to their dominant key. A minor key usually modulates to the relative major:

262. To counteract this, the after-phrase will swing towards the key one stage flatter than the tonic before returning home:

263. This may be expressed as follows: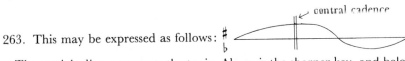

The straight line represents the tonic. Above is the sharper key, and below is the flatter key. The melody moves sharp first, and then passing through the tonic, it moves flatter before coming back to the tonic. The sharper key is the dominant in paragraph 261 and the flatter one is the subdominant in paragraph 262. The central cadence will always be at the sharpest point.

264. Relating this to the circle of keys, it will be seen which keys are involved in the design:

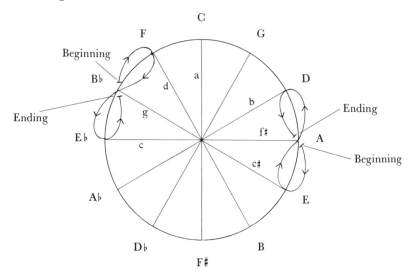

Any key centre may be taken as the tonic. The one on the left of the circle centred round B flat is the tonal scheme of the Bach melody above, the one on the right centred round A is the scheme of the Schubert song quoted below. This latter commences in A major and moves first to E major (it could touch C sharp minor too); it then returns through the tonic, (it could well have touched the relative minor, F sharp minor) to D major and thence home to A major:

265. After the central cadence in the dominant, the return via the sub-dominant may be rapid and many melodies achieve it by means of SEQUENCES.

There are two basic kinds of sequence:

TONAL SEQUENCES are repetitions of a phrase at different pitches but without chromatic change, that is, with the quality of the intervals changed to keep the passage diatonic:

REAL SEQUENCES are repetitions of phrases at different pitches but with the notes chromatically altered so that the intervals correspond in quality with the originals, semitone for semitone and wholetone for wholetone, etc. This involves momentary change of key. In this example, the first repetition is a real sequence, the second a tonal one:

Sequences, even when they are real ones, do not modulate firmly into other keys; they really give a momentary flavour of a key, which is a transition through it rather than an establishment of it:

and

etc.

Note that it takes more than a perfect cadence in a key to effect a firm modulation.

266. A move to a key can be made very much more conclusive if the two keys are linked by one of two methods:

(a) by moving from a chord in the first key but not in the second to a chord in the second key but not in the first, the two keys having one or more notes in common:

Mozart: *K. 457*

etc.

Note the Common B♭ in B♭ major and G♭ major

(b) by moving from a chord that is in both keys to the cadential harmony of the new key; this method is the most conclusive of all:

J. S. Bach

B♭ I   IV   Ib   V   VI   VII⁷b
Gm I   II⁷b   V   VI

Where the chords marked **X** are both common to B♭ major and G minor

267. Method (a) is known as modulation by a PIVOT NOTE; method (b) as modulation by a PIVOT CHORD.

268. The following sequence of chords reaches a pivot chord at + and thereafter is in the new key:

D mi.   I   V   I   IVb
F   IIb   Ib   V   I

269. A flowing bass sentence within this chord basis and closing in the new key would be:

D mi.   I ———————————— V ——— I   I   IVb
or   I   VIIb   Ib   IV   V ——— I   F   IIb   Ib   V   I

This version is slightly smoother and fills up some of the spaces in the second half with passing notes, which may or may not be harmonised:

D mi.   I   VIIb   Ib   IV   V ——— I ——— I   Vb   IVb
F   IIb   Ib   Vb   I   Ib   V   I

270. A melody that lies well above this bass is:

J. S. Bach

271. If it is required to write a melody to a bass or a bass to a melody, it is a waste of time to attempt the solution without discovering the implied harmony of the given part. In your early efforts always write it down and stick to it if possible.

272. Keys are said to be "related" when the tonic chord of each can be formed from the notes of the scale of the other. Thus the keys that are related to C major are those whose tonic chords may be formed from the notes of the scale of C major. They are:

Minors, D, E, A.
Majors, F, G.

273. The pivot chords between any of these keys and C may be found by comparing their scales. Those between C and D minor are:

The chords in brackets are a little ambiguous in use since they depend on the use of the notes of the melodic minor scale. As long as care is exercised in the use of the notes concerned, they may be used freely as pivots.

Those between C and E minor are:

Those between C and F major are:

Those between C and G major are:

Those between C and A minor are:

274. One or two examples will make clear what is involved.

To modulate from G major to A minor, a suitable chord succession would be:

A bass which lies within it:

A melody which also fits into it:

J. S. Bach

To modulate from G minor to E flat major: Chords in common are:

A suitable succession of chords:

A bass which lies within it:

A melody which also fits into it:

J. S. Bach

Notice that the appearance of the new leading note in either part confirms the modulation.

HARMONIC PROGRESSION

275. A succession of chords which leads naturally from one to another is called a CHORD PROGRESSION, but not all sequences of chords make a satisfactory progression.

276. Chords in root position on adjacent roots are seldom satisfactory, e.g. I-II:

This is weak and dull.

The same progression is strong and interesting if one of the chords is in 1st inversion position:

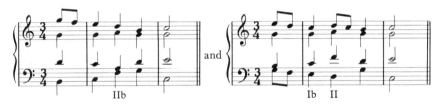

277. Chords whose roots are a 4th or a 5th apart always connect well:

This progression lies behind many of the sequential passages in Bach:

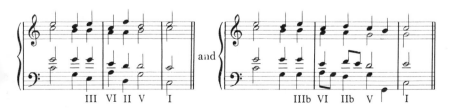

278. Occasionally chords that sound well in juxtaposition moving from strong beat to weak are unsatisfactory moving from weak to strong. For example II-IV, and VIIb-V:

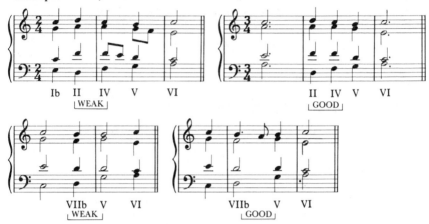

This sort of thing is best discovered at the keyboard by experiment. The use of inverted positions of the triads often relieves the weakness, as does a powerfully characteristic bass movement.

279. The second inversion chord needs care in its use. It functions most satisfactorily at a cadence (CADENTIAL SIX-FOUR), when, if its bass note is the dominant, it may be used on strong beats, the 6th resolving to a 5th, and the 4th to a 3rd.

280. Otherwise its use is best confined to weak beats with stepwise movement in approaching and quitting the bass note.

A common use of it is as a so-called PASSING SIX-FOUR between I and Ib, or IV and IVb, thus:

The $\frac{6}{4}$ in the penultimate bar is a cadential one. But even here, the Vc in the first bar is better replaced with VIIb:

VIIb

HARMONY—CHORDS OF THE SEVENTH

281. But now examine these perfect cadences:

In both examples you will find that the dominant note falls through a passing note to the 3rd of the tonic chord, and that there is a moment when the dominant chord sounds much enriched. The passing note forms the interval of a 7th with the root of the dominant. The sound at that moment is called the DOMINANT SEVENTH chord. Notice the movement of the individual notes:

(a) The 7th falls by step.

(b) The leading note rises a step as in the first example. Bach often allows it to fall a third in order to have a complete final chord.

282. The 7th may be sounded simultaneously with the dominant chord, thus:

283. The dominant seventh chord in root position is indicated by V7 and may also be figured 7 below the bass note.

284. The resolution of the seventh in the V^7 chord and its inversions needs care. The seventh above the root forms a discord with it and, like all discords, tends to resolve downwards:

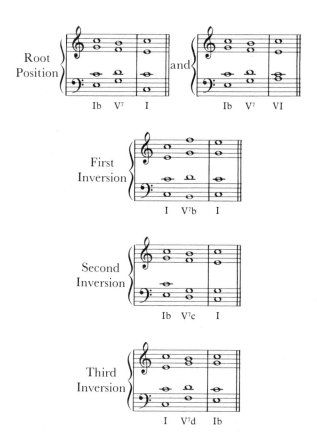

285. But note the possibility of the discordant seventh resolving upwards in the progression V^7c to Ib:

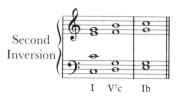

SEQUENCES

286. When, in a succession of chords, the roots of adjacent chords progress in a repeating pattern such as alternately up a fourth and down a fifth, the process is known as a SEQUENCE, for example, I—IV—VII—III—VI—II—V—I. There are many other progressions that can form sequences, but this is the only one we need to deal with here. It is a common sequence of chords in the music of Corelli, Vivaldi, Bach, Handel and practically all the masters of that period as well as in the work of all the "Classical" composers. Here is an example:

(a)

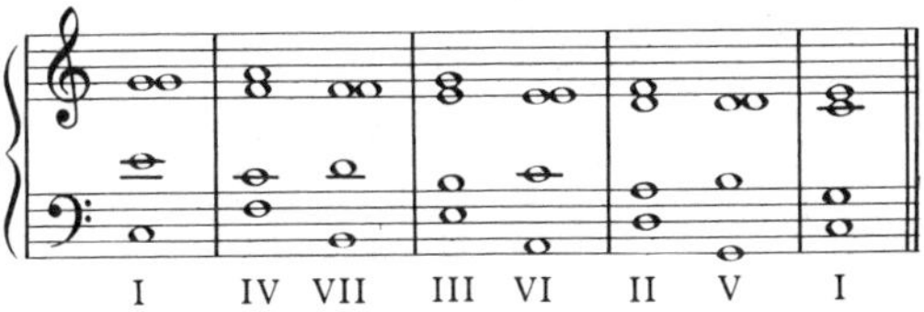

I   IV VII   III VI   II   V   I

The sequence works perfectly well when alternate chords are in first inversion:

(b)

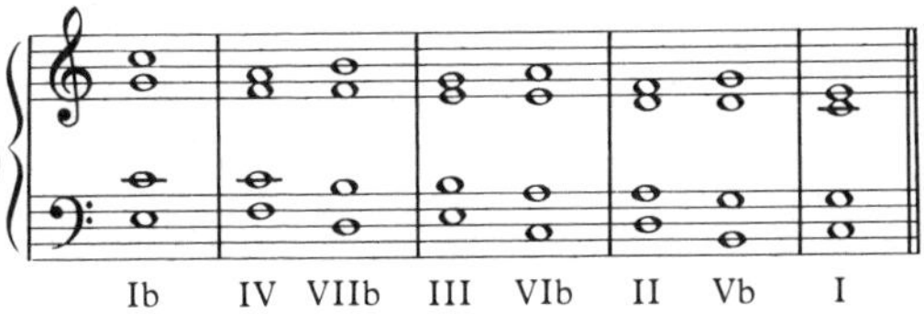

Ib   IV VIIb   III   VIb   II   Vb   I

287. Chromatic alteration of notes is possible and is an effective way of modulating to another key. For example, this modulates to D minor:

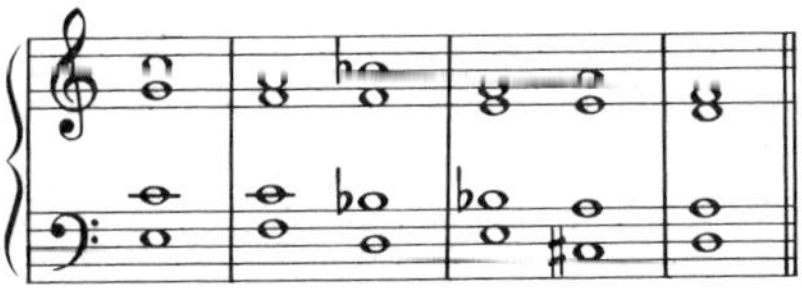

288. The 1st inversion of a triad always sounds the most interesting since it demands progress. It is perfectly possible to write a series of 1st inversions on adjacent bass notes with excellent effect:

Larghetto cantabile   Mozart: *Piano Concerto, K. 595*

Note that in 4 parts the tenor voice doubles alternately the 3rd and 6th, while the other parts move parallel with the bass; thus consecutives are avoided:

289. When harmonising a melody or bass in four parts, the individual voices or parts will not normally be as free and florid as those that are written for a piece in two parts, though the chorales of Bach will show that the style commonly associated with hymns is pretty dull stuff:

After Bach

J. S. Bach

Try to keep the inner parts, especially the tenor, interesting.

290. Spacing of parts too is important if euphony is to be achieved. Try to keep the tenor part high.

291. The chordal background is just as important when working in four parts as it is when working in two, and the bass line should always be most carefully considered in the chord implications it suggests. Always work to the cadences.

292. Four part harmony does not necessarily imply writing in continuous block chords. Here is a short melodic fragment harmonised in block chords; it is rather low for voices but it was not originally written for choir:

Now compare the following two styles of writing which make use of the same basic progression. The first is a flowing pianoforte style while the second is reduced to a three part texture. The first follows the four part version above exactly:

The medium for which you write must govern the style and texture in which you write; but however it is arranged, the basic harmony must be sound. Flowery arpeggios will not make a poor chord progression sound any better.

MINOR KEYS

293. The ambiguities of the minor scale make care necessary when you are writing in minor keys. A perfect cadence in a minor key necessitates a chromatic alteration of the 3rd of the dominant chord which is sharpened to make a true leading note. This leaves an augmented 2nd between the 6th and 7th degrees of the scale which often causes lack of smoothness in the individual parts; the melodic minor is therefore used to avoid the awkwardness.

294. The notes of the *harmonic* minor scale offer perfectly sound harmony provided that the chromatically raised leading note rises by step and that the flat 6th degree falls by step. This is always desirable. The following examples illustrate the only effective ways of using the top half of the melodic minor scale and should be carefully studied:

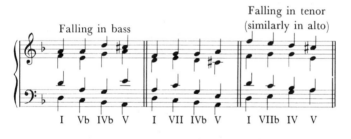

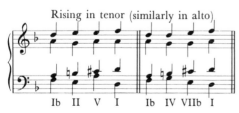

These examples illustrate the use of these resources in some chorales by Bach:

in bass

in treble

in alto

295. Chromatic alteration of the notes sometimes causes the effect of FALSE RELATIONS. If the same note appears in two consecutive chords but is chromatically altered in the second, it should be in the same part in both.

This is bad:

But if the altered note is the leading note of the new key, there is no ill effect:

If the altered note is the 7th of the "Dominant 7th" chord, there is also no ill effect.

The B in the treble in the first chord is followed by a B flat in the bass in the second, but it is the 7th of the dominant 7th of F major, and consequently sounds perfectly smooth.

HARMONIC ANALYSIS

296. The analysis of the harmony of a given passage should present no difficulty. In any texture there will be a true harmonic bass note; the only decisions that have to be made are concerned with:

    (a) the duration of each chord

    (b) which are essential and which are unessential harmonic notes.

As regards (a), the presence of pedal marks (if the music is for piano), give a very good guide, and the bottom notes of arpeggio figures give the true bass. Repeated figures on different scale degrees may help in understanding the harmonic pattern. These are only suggestions and experience and experiment are the best aids.

CLOSE AND OPEN SCORE—TRANSPOSITION

297. REWRITING FROM OPEN TO CLOSE SCORE AND VICE VERSA has already been dealt with. Where transposition from key to key is also involved, it may be necessary to make a transposed version of the original in your first efforts, before rewriting it with different scoring, but practice should make this unnecessary.

MUSICAL HISTORY

298. It is impossible in the space of this short Handbook to deal adequately with such a comprehensive and complex matter as musical history. The few remarks given below simply suggest how to approach the subject. History is not a series of dates. The study of musical history must concern itself first and foremost with music itself and with the factors that inspired the great composers to write their works and to develop their individual styles.

The seventeenth century is largely dominated by vocal music, the most important forms being madrigal, motet, opera and—arising out of monody—the accompanied song. Instrumental music begins by imitating vocal styles in fantasia, fancy, canzona, ricercare. As violin playing develops, the solo sonata, the trio sonata and the concerto grosso become favoured structures. Important factors in the development of styles are the Reformation and Counter-reformation, the development of rationalist thinking and the growth of a wealthy class requiring entertainment.

The eighteenth century begins with the attempt to rationalise all musical techniques, and the growth of the inevitable reaction to it in a movement extolling, above all, the power of the imagination. Opera grows into a stylised form from which springs opera buffa and comic opera. The German

principalities establish their own orchestras and employ their own kapel-
meisters to write, among other things, symphonies—hundreds upon hundreds are written, performed and forgotten. The orchestra grows more
settled in its constitution and true orchestral style, as opposed to chamber
music styles, evolves. The piano appears on the scene, and the piano concerto. The events leading to the French Revolution bring a new sense of free-
dom into man's outlook and consequently he engages in a search for ideals.
Romanticism is born when he strives to express his feelings in his artistic
expression.

The nineteenth century is remarkable for the personal involvement of the
composer. The concert world develops and the virtuoso performer appears.
Composers are influenced by poetry and idealism, and by Nationalism in
Russia, in Germany and even in England. Music becomes more chromatic
with the striving towards more and more intensity of expression, until the
bounds of key sense are stretched to breaking point.

The twentieth century sees the growth of the Atonal principle, and composers divide into two camps, the serialists and the non-serialists. New
instruments appear and Jazz is taken seriously. The second world war
brings great technical development in electronic equipment and this in turn
provides the material for experiment in a new medium in works for the
concert room. Some composers try to set music free from all restrictions
while others attempt to tie every facet of it to the mathematical proportions
of a chosen row of notes.

In studying musical history, try and relate the composers and their works
to the social and political state of the world that gave them birth, so that
man's expression through the arts shall be understood; then the reasons for
the development of certain forms will be clear, and history, far from being a
dry-as-dust subject, as it is so often thought to be, will be alive and will shed
light on the music itself. "History is what you thought. It is what you can
remember."* You will only remember it if your interest is aroused, and the
only thing that can do that is music.

A useful short textbook which deals with these matters concisely is "Man
and His Music", by Harman and Mellers, while the "Oxford Companion to
Music" is a thoroughly sound and comprehensive book of reference.

* from "*1066 and All That*" by Sellars and Yeatman (Penguin).

Chapter VII

SETTING WORDS TO MUSIC

299. The writing of a melody to given words must now be dealt with. The simplest way to approach the problem is as follows:

(a) Mark the accented syllables by underlining them. Here are two verses of a well-known poem as an example:

Proud <u>Mai</u>sie is in the <u>wood</u>,   '<u>Tell</u> me, thou <u>bon</u>ny bird,
  <u>Walk</u>ing so <u>ear</u>ly;   <u>When</u> shall I <u>mar</u>ry me?'
Sweet <u>Rob</u>in sits on the <u>bush</u>   When six braw <u>gen</u>tlemen
  <u>Sing</u>ing so <u>rare</u>ly.   <u>Kirk</u>ward shall <u>car</u>ry ye.'

The accented syllables are underlined.

(b) The choice of triple or duple time is largely a matter of individual preference, but the character of the words will generally make the choice straightforward. For example, a vigorous march-like poem will not go well in $\frac{3}{4}$. As, however, the verses quoted above are not of this kind, we will try to set them in $\frac{3}{4}$.

(c) Now make a plan of a series of bars, giving yourself plenty of room, in $\frac{3}{4}$ time, and fit the words into it so that the accented syllables fall on strong beats. The other syllables will be fitted into the weaker beats, always bearing in mind their related stresses.

This is a possible solution:

(d) It now remains to write a tune in, or close to this rhythm. Try and decide where the climax of the verse is and reflect it in the tune by building up to a high note, or to a syncopation, or other means of melodic accent. Both are illustrated here:

300.   With practice, it will be possible to write a tune straight off, but that will only come when you respond to the natural rhythm and accentuation of the verse quite spontaneously.

301.   Remember that if a phrase of poetry does not commence with an accented syllable, the musical rhythm will commence with an anacrusis, as in the example given.

302.   Try to capture the mood of the words in your melody. Melodies that contain many leaps will not convey tranquillity,but a joyful text will require lively rhythm and a tune that can contain considerable movement by leap.

303.   Remember that wide leaps are difficult to sing and that they must lie within the bounds of good harmony, so it is necessary to plan the cadences at phrase endings and to have an approximate idea of the drift of the harmony.

304.   Here is the tune to the poem we have set with a few indications of the cadential harmony:

TWO PART COUNTERPOINT

305. Counterpoint is the term used when the different voices in a piece of
harmonic writing flow smoothly with the help of the use of passing notes,
appoggiaturas, suspensions and other melodic decorations. For example, if
we take the top and bottom voices of the chords in 286(b), we find:

If we introduce passing notes (PN), we find:

This is immediately more flowing.

In this one, passing notes (PN) and appoggiaturas (APP) are added; the
result is a more varied flow still in both parts.

In this one, various more elaborate figures decorate the line, always within the basic harmonic background:

The most important thing to remember is that counterpoint or contrapuntal writing will only be effective if there is complete control of a logical progression of harmonies, and if there is some recognisable pattern in the decorative figures. But when the harmony is sequential, it is better to preserve sequences in the patterns of decoration. The last example is rather uncoordinated in melodic shape. It is no more than a demonstration of various possibilities.

In a piece of music in two parts, such as the second example in para. 305, if we put the bass line up an octave and the treble line down an octave, the result is just as musical as the original:

This is known as INVERSION and is a useful and common procedure in two part writing. Refer to Bach's Two Part Inventions for copious examples.

DANCES IN TWO PARTS

306.   Points to watch in completing dances in two parts are:

(a) Do not lose sight of your cadence points.

(b) Make sure that the harmony, when it changes, does so on strong beats, especially if it has just changed on a weak beat.

307. Here is a straightforward Minuet by Bach:

The first sentence of this contains 4 phrases of which the 1st and 3rd are the same. The 2nd phrase ends with an imperfect cadence I-V, the 1st and 3rd also end in imperfect cadences, but they are IVb (or VI)-V. The 4th phrase modulates straightaway through C minor into B flat and ends there with a perfect cadence. The 5th phrase, the 1st after the double bar, starts off in B flat and moves to F major where there is a not-very-conclusive perfect cadence. The 6th phrase contradicts F and returns to B flat and makes a perfect cadence there, but the bass moves through it and the music makes no stop. The 7th phrase makes an inverted cadence into C minor, on the subdominant side of the home key, and then finishes with an imperfect cadence on the home dominant, G minor, thus C minor has been used as a modulating pivot between B flat major and G minor. The last phrase ends with a firm and punctual perfect cadence in G minor. There is a climax of high notes in the 5th phrase made more bright by being in the sharpest key touched upon in the piece.

Notice the sequences in the 2nd phrase, and the tendency of the 7th phrase to commence with two single bar phrases.

308. Try to avoid the effect of stagnation when both parts reach long notes simultaneously. This is perfectly sound writing from the harmonic point of view, but lacks rhythmic interest at (X):

Interest is kept up by keeping one part moving:

Study the "Anna Magdalene" book of Bach to see the sort of melodic fillers he uses.

This sort of thing is also useful for preventing the movement from coming to a premature stop:

309. The form in which the majority of the dances are cast is known as
B I N A R Y form since the whole dance divides into two parts with a half
close in the middle or with a modulation to a key on the sharp side of the
tonic. There is generally a double bar at the half way and the direction to
repeat each half. If there is no clear-cut pause in the middle, the piece
acquires the continuity of a TWO-PART INVENTION. The cadence points are
there, but they are undermined by movement in one or other of the voices.
Examine the Two-part Inventions of Bach in illustration of this, but you will
not be expected to work on this scale at this stage.

HARMONY—CHORDS OF THE SEVENTH

310. In the same way as a 7th may be used with the dominant chord to
form the chord of the dominant 7th, so a 7th may be added to any other
chord. The resulting chords are called SECONDARY SEVENTHS.

311. Here are the root positions of all the secondary 7ths in C major with
their following chords of resolution:

I^7 IV II^7 V III^7 VI IV^7 VII VI^7 II VII^7 III

Note that the 7th from the root always falls by step to the note of resolution,
the 3rd of the following chord.

312. These chords are all usable in inverted positions:

I^7d II^7b III^7c   etc.

The first inversion of the secondary 7th on the supertonic is known as the
chord of the ADDED SIXTH:

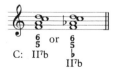

$\begin{smallmatrix}6\\5\end{smallmatrix}$ or $\begin{smallmatrix}6\\5\end{smallmatrix}$

C: II^7b $\flat$
              II^7b

313. The chord that precedes the secondary 7th may be any chord that sounds well with it.

314. It is not necessary for 7th chords to resolve as above; any chord may be used to follow them that sounds well, but it should be noted that the voice that has the 7th will not normally proceed by leap. Here are some examples of other resolutions:

I⁷c VI⁷d VII⁷c III⁷   I⁷b II⁷b

Schumann: Song, *Ich grolle nicht*

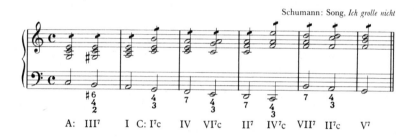

A: III⁷   I C: I⁷c   IV   VI⁷c   II⁷   IV⁷c VII⁷ II⁷c   V⁷

315. When writing in two parts, the 7th chord will only be implied if the root and the 7th are present:

V ———— V⁷   and   II⁷d VII ——— V⁷

But note that in flowing two-part counterpoint, the resolution of the 7th may not be immediate, although it must take place eventually:

V   V⁷——————————— I

316. II⁷, IV⁷ and VII⁷ may conveniently be used before a perfect or interrupted cadence:

317. A common approach to a seventh chord is from a triad whose root is a third higher. Thus a cadence on the dominant at the half-way point or at the end of a phrase can be followed with very strong effect by III⁷, the bass merely falling a 3rd:

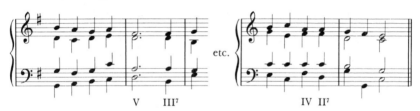

THE PRINCIPAL ORCHESTRAL INSTRUMENTS

STRING TECHNIQUE

318. The Violin. The most expressive of all the instruments.

Four strings tuned: Compass:

G string is very warm and rich in tone.

Very expressive throughout its entire compass.

Chords of 2, 3 or even 4 notes may be played, but the limited compass of the hand must be borne in mind when attempting to write what is called double, triple or quadruple stops—consult a good manual or preferably a violinist about this.

The violin may be muted; the tone then becomes veiled and acquires a slight edge. This is indicated by the words CON SORDINO.

The violin is normally played with a bow, but it may also be played "PIZZICATO" by plucking the strings with the fingers. The tone is very short-lived in pizzicato. Another effect, COL LEGNO, is obtained by striking the strings with the wood of the bow.

Chord positions may be effectively arpeggiated across the strings:

Very wide legato leaps across the strings are difficult if not impossible since they involve crossing strings without sounding them. Wide staccato leaps are brilliantly effective.

Playing on or near the bridge alters the tone considerably; in *f*, it becomes strident and harsh, in *p*, it is glassy and weird. This is known as PONTICELLO and indicated by writing against the passage to be so played "SUL. PONT.".

319.   The Viola.

A dark, rather nasal quality of tone.

Not always effective as a solo instrument as its tone does not possess very assertive qualities. The general remarks about the violin are also applicable to the viola.

320.   The Violoncello—'Cello for short.

A warm toned bass to the string quartet and a perfectly adequate bass to the orchestra except in *ff*.

The A string is very full and rich and on it over two octaves of range is available. A little slower to speak than the violin, it is still very agile and the general remarks about the violin also apply to the 'cello.

321.   The Double Bass.

The bass of the orchestra.

Tone is dry in solo and its use as such is often in terms of the grotesque. Sounds an octave lower than written:

322.   It is not normal practice to mark all the lengths of the phrases, as it is generally assumed that a player will have the necessary musicianship to feel when phrases begin and end. Instead, slurs and dots are used to mark "bowing". So far as strings are concerned, the character of the musical performance depends upon style and method of using the bow.

The slur is used to indicate what notes are to be played with one stroke of the bow. When notes are to be detached from one another, as in the music of Bach and Handel, no slur is used. If they are to be played staccato they are marked with dots or dashes. If a series of notes are to be played legato, they may be grouped under a slur if there are not too many of them, and played without changing the direction of the bow stroke. But note that a good violinist can play notes legato even though he does change the direction of his bow stroke.

If notes are slurred and also marked with dots, they are played with one bow stroke, but the bow is nearly stopped or lifted off the string between each note, making them slightly detached.

This example shows all these effects:

Brahms: *Violin Concerto*

323.   Different parts of the bow produce different qualities and effects:

Point  Heel

(a) Playing at the heel produces firm full tone and accents.

(b) Playing at the point produces lighter and smoother tone.

324.   When the bow is moved so that the part in contact with the string moves from point to heel, it is easy to obtain a crescendo to an accent on the change of bow. Moving the bow in this direction is called an UP BOW and the sign for it is V above a note.

325.   It is generally desirable to contrive the bowing so that there is a change of bow from up to down, or on occasion down to up, on the strong beats, thus:

Allegro moderato

Tschaikowsky: *Symphony No. 5*

A good violinist can accent with either up or down bow.

326.   The sign for a down bow stroke is ⊓ , but both ⊓ and V are seldom used, the initiative being left to the player.

327. To accent strongly single notes that are not played too fast, it is possible to bow them thus:

in which case the player lifts the bow off after each note and plays the next with a down bow starting at the heel.

328. As a string player can play a very considerable number of notes without changing the bow, do not be afraid to write a passage of this type:

But if you want loud tone, there are limits to the number of notes playable on one bow:

The first example in "*p*" is good, but in "*f*" it would have to be broken as in the second.

329. The best way of finding out all the effects of different bowings is to get a friendly violinist to show you. The subtleties of string bowing are enormous, and only the vaguest general principles can be mentioned here.

330. The following types of bowing are common in semiquaver passages in the classics:

WOODWIND

331. Slurs and dots are used here also to mark legato and staccato. The player "tongues" each note unless it is joined to another with a slur. The tonguing gives an accent to the note.

102

332. Do not expect long legato passages from your wind instruments; the player must have moments to breathe.

333. Legato is made difficult by changes of register, certain awkward fingerings, and by wide leaps in the brass.

334. The flute and the brass instruments can reiterate repeated notes more quickly than the clarinet, oboe and bassoon, specially the two last.

335. The flute uses a great deal of breath, more than any other woodwind instrument and long unbroken phrases are a considerable strain. The oboe uses very little and this creates a different problem; an oboist must be given time to exhale as well as inhale.

336. This may seem an obvious point, but remember that in *ff* much more breath is used.

PIANOFORTE

337. In writing for the piano, care should be taken over the use of slurs. In much romantic and modern music, but not in Brahms, the slur is commonly used to indicate beginnings and endings of phrases, details of articulation being added as well. In the classics the slur marks legato, and corresponds exactly with bowing. Used in conjunction with staccato dots as in

 it indicates that the second semiquaver is made staccato. Similarly

the final note of a group is shortened before a rest.

When the slur is used to group notes in a legato melody as in Beethoven's Sonata Op. 13 in the Adagio, it indicates that a fresh downward movement of the hand is required at the beginning of the 3rd bar:

Adagio cantabile · Beethoven: *Sonata, Op. 13*

but without breaking the legato. Compare bowing: a change of bow does not necessarily mean a break of tone. In the example quoted, the D flat is an up-beat to the C and the downward movement of the hand will accent the C very slightly. Beethoven knew what he wanted and how to get it, and editors who change these things do violence to the composer's style.

It will be seen, therefore, that in the classics, slurs do not necessarily indicate beginnings and endings of phrases.

INSTRUMENTAL COLOURS AND CAPABILITIES

338. Full information about this complex matter is best sought in one of the standard manuals of orchestration. Here, it will have to suffice to give only the barest indications.

339. Flute.

Compass:

Low notes have little weight and are easily swamped.
Very shrill in the topmost octave.
Clear and unemotional tone quality.
Very agile.

340. Oboe.

Compass: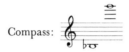

Low notes are very powerful and hard to play softly.

Upper two octaves very flexible and expressive.

Tone has a reedy edge and can be plaintive, pastoral or very full of emotion.

Fairly agile.

It has a double reed.

341. Clarinet.

Compass:  written notes

Lowest octave can be hollow and sepulchral. Very useful for "Alberti"* type accompaniment figures. See the trio in the third movement of Mozart's *Symphony in E flat* No. 39.

* Domenico Alberti, 1710-1740, is chiefly remembered by an accompaniment formula of the type shown in the following example. He used this excessively and it is commonly known as the Alberti Bass. Many examples will be found in the works of Haydn and Mozart.

 etc.

From the B above middle C the tone is full and expressive.

Very agile; rapid scales and arpeggios fairly simple.

Topmost octave hard and military.

It has a single reed.

The tone quality of the clarinet derives from the fact that certain overtones are missing from its harmonic series and, as a consequence, the instrument's natural second octave up, normally produced by overblowing at the octave, is actually the result of its overblowing at the 12th. This leaves a gap between the top of the lowest octave and the bottom of the singing register which has to be filled by extra keys. This gap is known as "the break" and extends from F above middle C to the B flat above it. In the hands of a good player there is little or no change of tone colour, but these notes are not easy to produce and in writing important solo parts they should be avoided.

The clarinet is a "transposing instrument", that is, it plays a different pitch from the notes written for it. It is made in several different sizes, but only two are in normal use, the B flat and A clarinets. A player on the B flat clarinet, seeing a scale of C, will play one sounding in B flat, and an instrument in A, with exactly the same fingering, will play one sounding in A. Thus, to write for the B flat clarinet, it is necessary to write a whole tone above the notes required and to put two fewer flats or two more sharps into the key signature. Similarly to write for the clarinet in A, it is necessary to write a minor 3rd above the required notes and to write three more flats or three fewer sharps in the key signature.

An example will make this clear:

342. The Bassoon.

Compass:

A reedy and powerful bass.

Agile, specially in leaps from high notes to low ones and vice-versa.

Cross fingering makes some notes and some scales difficult. Consult a good manual.

It has a double reed.

BRASS

343. The French Horn.

Compass:  written notes

A warm toned instrument, capable of very expressive playing.

Not very agile.

Very effective as a soft background with long held notes.

Notes can be stopped or overblown, producing a strident brassy sound. When this is required, they are marked with a cross (+) above them.

It has 3 valves which lower the pitch 1 tone, ½ tone, 1½ tones, in that order.

The modern horn, like the trumpet, is chromatic throughout its compass, but before valves were invented, the notes a player could produce were only those of the harmonic series; this confined the instrument to one key. When the composer wanted a special key, he prescribed the use of a "crook" in that key. A crook was a length of brass tubing that tuned the instrument to the required key. Nowadays horn music is generally written for horn in F, in which case it transposes a 5th down:

344. The Trumpet.

Compass

A brilliantly toned instrument that cannot conceal its prominence in a texture even when played softly.

Like the horn, it is now chromatic throughout its compass.

Useful for marking rhythm, but also very effective as a melody instrument.

Agile.

Like the Horn, it has 3 valves.

345. Trombones. 2 sizes.

Tenor. Compass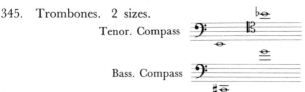

Bass. Compass

Brilliant and warm in tone.

Effective in climax.

The sound of a group of trombones softly played and spaced closely together is threatening, but very sonorous if the notes are widely spaced.

Useful as a solo instrument, but the ear tires of the sound if it is overused.

Certain "pedal" notes are available to a good player below the given compass—consult a good manual on this point.

346. Tuba.

Normal Compass

in F

A thick enveloping tone quality.

Very useful as a bass in a big climax.

Grotesque as a solo instrument.

It has 3–5 valves, depending on size and type.

347. Mutes. The tone of the horn, trumpet, trombone and tuba is considerably altered when mutes are used with them (indicated by "con sordini").

When muted, the horn can be the softest sound in the orchestra, but played loudly it acquires a strident edge.

The trumpet muted sounds thin and almost tinny, and is very penetrating.

Trombones muted become veiled and distant.

The tuba muted is much softer and less oily.

348. Accidentals in brass parts.

In the classics it was normal practice to write without key signatures, adding the accidentals as required. Nowadays key signatures are freely used. Thus a horn in F playing in the key of F will have no key signature, horn in F playing in A flat will have 3 flats in the key signature, horn in F playing in A will have 4 sharps in the key signature. Horn in F will have one less flat or one more sharp than the non-transposing instruments.

Trumpets are often written for in C in which case they sound as written, but if they are written for in B flat, they are like the clarinet in B flat and sound a whole tone lower than written.

349. The only other transposing instruments in common use are:
Piccolo, which sounds an octave higher than written.

Compass

Cor Anglais, a kind of tenor oboe that sounds a 5th below the written notes and like the horn in F requires one flat less or one sharp more in the key signature.

Compass  written notes

The Double Bassoon, sounding an octave lower than written.

Compass 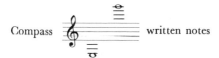 written notes

Bass clarinet in B flat sounding a 9th lower than written.

Compass  written notes

350. The rewriting from open to close score or vice-versa presents no problem not already dealt with except the added complication involved in the use of transposing instruments.

Here is the second example quoted in para. 193 arranged for Oboe and Clarinet in B flat.

and for Clarinet in A and Cor Anglais:

and for Horn in F and Trumpet in B flat:

Here is the first example from the same paragraph arranged for Oboe, Cor Anglais, Clarinet in A and Bassoon.

In your first efforts at rewriting, it may be best to do the work in two stages: first rewrite in terms of the actual sounds, then rewrite again using the prescribed instruments.

Chapter VIII

THE CHROMATIC SCALE

351. A chromatic scale is one in which all the steps are semitones.

352. There are two forms of this scale, the HARMONIC CHROMATIC SCALE, so called because from its notes all the chromatic harmonies and chords may be formed, and the MELODIC CHROMATIC SCALE in which the notes are sharpened in rising and flattened in descending with the exception of the augmented fourth from the key note which is sharpened in both.

353. The harmonic chromatic scale is formed thus:
    To the notes of the major scale (shown here for convenience in semibreves) add the notes that are also found in the minor scales—both forms (in minims):

To this add the flattened second above the tonic and the sharpened fourth above the tonic (in crotchets):

354. When using the minor key signature add to the notes of the minor scale those found in the major scale, also the flattened second and the augmented fourth above the key note as before:

355. The descending form is the same as the ascending:

356. In the melodic chromatic scale the notes are sharpened going up:

in E♭

and flattened descending except for the augmented fourth from the key note marked with a (X):

in F♯

This is identical with the descending harmonic chromatic scale, and so it is generally said that the melodic chromatic scale is a rising form only. If the scale is written descending with the minor key signature, it becomes somewhat complicated around the note a fourth above the tonic and so is not used descending. In any case the profusion of flats in this example dispels any feeling for key:

in E

INTERVALS

357.   The harmonic chromatic scale introduces some intervals within the compass of the octave that have not yet been encountered as well as the obvious duplication of by now familiar ones. Here is the harmonic chromatic scale of C over two octaves:

It will be seen that the following intervals in addition to the ones already listed in chapter IV paragraph 168 ff can be formed from its notes:

Augmented 2nd	D flat—E, E flat—F sharp,
Diminished 3rd	F sharp—A flat, B natural—D flat,
Augmented 3rd	D flat—F sharp,
Diminished 4th	F sharp—B flat, A—D flat,
Augmented 4th	C—F sharp, D flat—G,
Diminished 5th	F sharp—C, G—D flat,
Augmented 5th	D flat—A natural, B flat—F sharp,
Diminished 6th	F sharp—D flat,
Augmented 6th	A flat—F sharp, D flat—B natural,
Diminished 7th	F sharp—E flat, E—D flat.

358.   Note the chromatic and diatonic semitones throughout this scale:

Chromatic 2nd	D flat—D natural
	E flat—E natural
	F—F sharp
	A flat—A natural
	B flat—B natural
Diatonic 2nd	C—D flat
	D natural—E flat
	E natural—F
	F sharp—G
	G—A flat
	A natural—B flat
	B natural—C.

359. As the harmonic chromatic scale is the principal one in use, it is not thought necessary to list here all the possible intervals in the melodic form, though these may easily be discovered by the student for himself should he so wish.

360. A study of the intervals given above and in earlier chapters will show that it is not possible to state definitely the key of an interval, specially if it is a simple diatonic one, since every interval may be found in at least two keys. For instance this interval

may be found in C major, F major, B flat major, E flat major, D minor, C minor, F minor, G minor, A minor—remembering both forms of the minor scale.

This interval, however, only appears in the scales of B and E harmonic chromatic:

CHROMATIC HARMONY

361. Diatonic harmony can be made more vivid and sensuous by the chromatic alteration of some of the notes in the chords. In theory, there is no limit to the amount of chromatic alteration possible, but it must be remembered that too much indiscriminate use will undermine the sense of key, an effect deliberately used by Wagner in *Tristan* and *Parsifal*, and more especially by Mahler, Reger and Strauss.

Here we must confine our attention to the use of chromaticism which

(a) does not undermine tonality and

(b) effects clear modulation, even if only temporarily.

362. The commonest chromatic chords in use in any key may be grouped under the heading SECONDARY DOMINANTS. The dominant chords of the keys that are the direct relations to any one key centre are known as secondary dominants, and their momentary use in no way upsets the basic tonality. In these examples, the secondary dominants are marked with a cross (+):

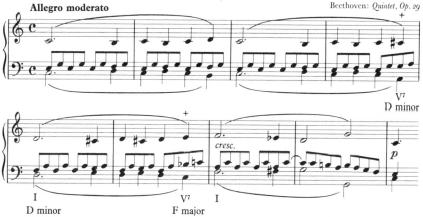

Allegro moderato

Beethoven: *Quintet, Op. 29*

363. The major chord on the supertonic of a key is one such secondary dominant. This example is in C major.

Care must be taken in vocal music not to allow any chromatic alteration to make a part jump awkward augmented intervals; so watch the approach to chromatically altered notes.

364. THE AUGMENTED TRIAD.

Sharpening the 5th of a major chord is one of the commonest chromatic alterations. The resultant augmented triad will tend to resolve onto a chord whose root is a 4th above its own:

Observe that the chromatically altered note rises by a semitone. It will be found that chromatically altered notes resolve most satisfactorily by step, sharpened ones upwards and flattened ones downwards.

365. Notice this perfect cadence in which the 5th of the dominant chord is sharpened:

Here is the same cadence with a 7th added to the chromatically altered dominant chord.

366. Notice this perfect cadence in which the 5th of the dominant chord is flattened, also with the 7th present:

This chord is identical with one discussed below (376 ff).

367. This progression is common:

In a minor key it is:

Flattening of the 6th above the bass makes the progression much more tragically expressive:

This chord is known as the NEAPOLITAN SIXTH and is available in both major and minor keys.

Examples:

368. The use of the chords derived from a minor key in its tonic major is part of the normal harmonic language of Beethoven and Schubert. Examples of the application of this principle are:

Minor chord on IV:

Major chord on flat III:

Major chord on flat VI:

369. The reverse procedure using chords derived from a major key in its tonic minor is not always convincing; but provided that the raised notes can be treated as part of the melodic minor scale, there should be no trouble:

It will be found that the chords I and III from the major key are difficult to use in the minor. I major tends to effect a temporary shift into the key of the subdominant, and III simply sounds wrong in any context.

370. These are common progressions:

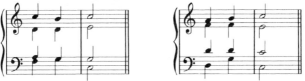

Sharpening of the bass of the IIb in the former and the 3rd of the II in the latter produces a brightened progression. The chord is the dominant of the dominant, but a modulation to the key of the dominant is not so easily effected and the use of this chord does not undermine tonality:

371. An interesting sound emerges if the 5th above the root of this chord is flattened, especially if a 7th above the root is added too. This will be discussed in para. 376.

372. The minor IV may be used freely in a plagal cadence in a major key:

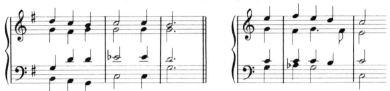

This merely makes the cadence more expressive.

373. Sharpening the root of this chord produces another interesting sound, dealt with in the next paragraph:

374. The progression IVb-V is a common enough one in both major and minor keys, and the minor IVb is powerful and expressive when used in the major. Using the flattened 6th degree of the scale and raising the 6th above it a chromatic semitone in no way alters the basic tread of chords but enhances enormously the expressive nature of it. This chord is known as the AUGMENTED SIXTH, ITALIAN VERSION; the interval of the augmented sixth lies between the A flat and the F sharp in the first example and between the E flat and the C sharp in the second example:

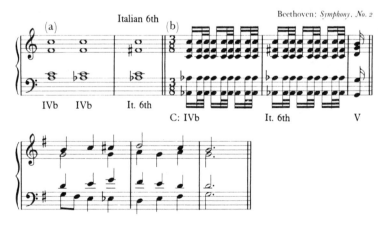

375. If the chord mentioned in para. 373 is compared with the Italian augmented 6th, it will be seen that it is an inversion of it.

376. If the chords mentioned in paragraphs 371 and 373 are combined (note that their treatment can be identical), the chord that results is known as the FRENCH SIXTH. This is another form of augmented 6th chord:

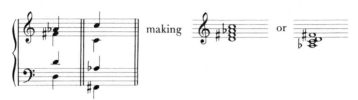

Note that this chord is a chromatically altered added 6th chord:

377. If, to the chord of flat VI an augmented 6th is added, the resulting chord is known as the GERMAN sixth. Note that this sounds the same as a dominant 7th chord in another key:

Note also the consecutive fifths between Alto and Bass. In this particular progression, these are quite acceptable as they do not sound prominent. Examples are common.

378. These augmented 6th chords, Italian, French and German are built on the flattened 6th degree of the scale. They may also lie on the flattened 2nd:

379. Note that if the German 6th is treated as a dominant 7th and resolved as such, the key that it resolves into is the flat supertonic, whose tonic chord in 1st inversion position is the Neapolitan 6th in the original key. This is only mentioned to show how these highly coloured harmonies are intimately related to one another and are often used to enhance the expressiveness of the approach to the cadence:

G   I   Vb   IVb   G 6   N6   V ——— I
            Ab   V⁷   I   Ib

380. Any minor triad may be converted into a diminished triad by flattening its 5th. The altered note will resolve downwards:

381. Similarly any major chord may be changed into a diminished one by sharpening its root, and this altered note will resolve upwards:

382. Note this chord:

This is identical in sound on the piano with this:

The resolutions are not the same:

383. The addition of an A to either chord converts into diminished 7ths. Note the resolutions:

and note this one:

The ear will accept each for the other, but it makes for simpler notation if a flattened note falls and a sharpened one rises and this is more grammatical.

384. Diminished 7ths are usable on every note of the chromatic scale and the ear is the only arbiter of their suitability:

385. Diminished 7ths may resolve by resolution downwards one semitone of any one of its notes. Observe the enharmonic change of some of the notes in these; the resulting chords will sound like dominant 7ths and may be so treated, in which case the diminished 7th chord acts like a pivot:

386. The unrestricted use of chromatic chords tends to undermine the key. To avoid this, they should be followed by chords that are diatonic in the key.

387. The addition of a minor 7th to a major tonic chord is a commonly used chromatic alteration, but it must be followed by a chord in which the chromatic change is cancelled. Note the following string of chords:

Here a number of them are connected in a logical sequence.

388. Some examples of their use in actual music:

389. Just as diatonic harmony is constantly enriched by the use of appoggiaturas, suspensions and passing notes, so it is often enriched by chromatic appoggiaturas, etc., and the chromatic chords themselves are often enriched by similar use of embellishments of various kinds:

Strauss: *Till Eulenspiegel*

here the D flat is a chromatic appoggiatura to the root of the chromatically altered dominant chord.

390. It must be realised that this is the language of the Romantic composers, and that anything resembling the example in para. 389 is beyond the range of Mozart or Haydn. The chorales of Bach often offer remarkable examples of the use of chromatic chords; in the miraculous end of the "Crucifixus" of Bach's *B minor Mass*, the special colour of the chords captures uniquely the meaning of the text:

J. S. Bach: *Mass in B minor*

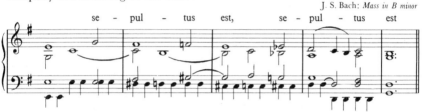

391. All chromatic chords are available as modulatory pivots, and the two Wolf songs quoted above show their use as such. The choral writing and songs of Brahms, Parry, Stanford and others also show fine use of their resources.

FURTHER DISCORDS

392. Another class of discords must be referred to—the so-called 9ths, 11ths and 13ths, all generally embellishments of 7th chords.

These are best considered as examples of appoggiaturas to some of the notes of the chord. The dominant 9th is an appoggiatura to the root of the dominant chord:

(a)

or to the third of the same chord, resolving upwards;

Here it resolves onto chord I.

(b) The dominant 11th is an appoggiatura to the 3rd of the chord:

Here it resolves onto chord I.

(c) The dominant 13th is an appoggiatura to the 5th of the chord:

Here it resolves onto chord I. The essential notes which are displaced by the appoggiaturas are shown in brackets.

393.   Note that the 9th is figured 9, but the 11th and 13th are figured respectively 4 and 6 when the dominant chord is in root position. When it is not, the figuring must be counted from the bass.

but:

394. Major and minor 9ths and 13ths may be used freely in the major key.

395. Try to sound the major 9th above the 3rd of the chord if possible, as it is harsh if sounded below it. The minor 9th is effective above or below the 3rd.

It is best not to sound the note of resolution of these discords against the discords themselves, though it is sometimes perfectly acceptable if the note of resolution is in the bass as in the second example.

Not good

Perfectly good

CHORALES IN THE STYLE OF J. S. BACH

396. The writing of Chorales in the style of Bach is a very difficult task. The best way to tackle them is along these lines:

(a) Decide on the key of each phrase, particularly the one on which it ends.

(b) Sketch in the cadence, provisionally in root position chords.

(c) Complete the sketch in of all the basic harmony, seeing that the part writing is sound.

(d) Try and achieve smooth individual parts, using all the resources of auxiliary notes, appoggiaturas, anticipations, passing notes, suspensions.

(e) It may be necessary to alter the chord positions at the cadences in order to achieve smooth movement from one phrase to another.

124

Here are two examples which show:
  (a) the chorale melody
  (b) the keys and cadences
  (c) a straightforward harmonisation based on what Bach actually did
  (d) Bach's final version.

No. 366 O Welt, Sieh hier dein Leben

(c)

(d)

Notes: 1. The first and second phrases are repeated. N.B., the chords are not the same both times.
2. Mark the constant falling of the leading note by a third.
3. The sounding of a discord against its note of resolution in bars 5, 7 and 11.
4. The doubling of major thirds in bars 1, 3, 10, 11.
5. Several leaps of an octave—in bass and alto.
6. The crossing of alto and tenor in bar 8.
7. The occasional wide gaps between Soprano and Alto, bars 7-8, also between alto and tenor in bars 9-10.

These things are all contributory to the achievement of the maximum smoothness of the individual parts. There are three versions of this Chorale in the Riemenschneider collection, so that it cannot be said that there is any one right version, though there may well be faulty ones.

No. 134 Du, o schönes Weltgebände

Notes: 1. The third phrase is repeated. It could well be harmonised the second time in D minor with possibly an interrupted cadence. Note what Bach does.

2. Notice the consecutives at the cadence between tenor and bass.

3. Notice the apparent false relations in bar 12.

4. The third and fourth cadences are the same chords but in different positions.

COUNTERPOINT

397. So far, efforts at counterpoint in two parts have been straightforward and simple, and the two parts have complemented one another more or less as bass and treble are complementary. Now we have to consider a style where the two parts imitate one another. This is most clearly seen in some (but not all), of the dances in the French Suites of Bach, and more especially in the same composer's Two-part Inventions.

398. In this style the two voices are on a much more equal footing, instead of functioning as melody and bass. Here is the opening of the Gigue from the B minor French Suite:

J. S. Bach: *Gigue, French Suite in B minor*

399. Instead of a continuous flow of melody in one part supported by a flowing bass, the interest of the music passes to and fro between the parts in fairly rapid succession, especially at the beginning and at certain other moments in the composition. The melodic lines are constructed much more from short figures which re-appear in one voice after another, and the first voice to enter in this style often seems to pause and wait for the other.

400. Note that the two parts imitate, but not exactly. When the imitation is exact as regards scale steps, the parts are said to be in CANON. The *Two-part Invention in C minor* is in canon throughout at the interval of an octave, as are the first eight bars of that in F major.

401. Imitation is present in all these Inventions, but sometimes the imitating part fills up the beginning before commencing to imitate some distance from the beginning as in that in G minor:

J. S. Bach: *Two-part invention in G minor*

402.   Sometimes, as in those in D major and D minor, the second voice enters after a couple of bars of rests:

J. S. Bach: *Two-part invention in D*

Sometimes, as in that in C major, the second half of the first part's phrase acts as a counterpoint to the imitating voice which in this case enters half a bar after the first:

J. S. Bach: *Two-part invention in C*

403.   The use of imitation between the voices makes it very desirable that the two parts should be capable of INVERSION.

There are two kinds of inversion:

(a)   The notes of a melody may be inverted, in which case what went up in the original goes down in the inversion and vice-versa:

J. S. Bach: *C major invention*

(b)   When the two-part counterpoint is inverted, the part that was in the bass in the original appears in the treble, and the original treble appears in the bass.   The only points to watch are concerned with the inversion of intervals of 5ths and 4ths.

This sounds good: This would be rough:

Note the poor departure from a 4th at the beginning of the bar and the consecutive 5ths which would be rather too obvious in two parts.

130

Example:

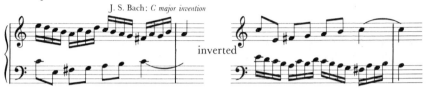

J. S. Bach: *C major invention*

inverted

404. Note that in none of these Inventions is constant imitation between the parts maintained throughout, as the examination of one of the Inventions in detail will show:

J. S. Bach: *Two-part invention in C*

405. Notes on *Two-part Invention No. 1 in C major:*

BARS 1-2. The first two bars are concerned with imitation between the two voices; note how the second half of the phrase is not the same in both.

BAR 3. A paragraph commences that modulates into G major and reaches a cadence in that key in bar 7. The sequential harmony of bars 3 and 4 is a logical harmonic progression that leads inexorably into the new key through the chord of A minor as a pivot in bar 4.

BAR 7. The imitation starts again in G major between the two parts.

BAR 9. The imitation here is of the inversion of the opening figure, the steps rising at each entry to reach D minor at bar 11.

BAR 11. From this point, the paragraph that started at bar 3 and led to G major at bar 7 is repeated with the parts inverted, treble in bass and bass in treble, leading from D minor to A minor in bar 15.

This use of a paragraph in another place and in different keys is common among the two-part Inventions. Compare the Invention in F major, bars 4-12 with bars 26-end.

BAR 15. The imitation starts again in A minor, passes through D minor, G major, C major and just touches F major, the subdominant, before effecting the close in C major. The passage beginning in 19 is like that commencing in bar 3 with the individual parts inverted in direction but with the pair of parts corresponding, that is, semiquavers in the right-hand part in both.

406. Close examination of the Inventions and dances of both Bach and Handel is recommended.

407. The dances generally come to a clearer cadence at the halfway in the dominant or related key.

It is a good plan when writing in dance forms to close both halves with the same sentence, in the related key the first time and in the tonic the second.

Examine the following passages by Bach:

French Suite in E
Bourrée, last 4 bars of each section
Courante, last 5 bars of each section
Allemande, last 4 bars of first section and last 7 of the second—there is a coda.

French Suite in G
Courante, last 4 bars of each section

French Suite in B minor
Gigue, last 8 bars of each section.

THE TEXTURE OF PIANO MUSIC

408. In writing for piano, several points must be remembered:

(a) The tone of the piano quickly fades.

(b) The compass of the hands is limited, and so writing is bound to be sketchy to some extent.

(c) The sustaining pedal will help to hold harmonic background and also to fill up the gaps between the hands.

(d) Never forget the relationship between the melodic line and the true harmonic bass even though the actual notes of the bass are no longer sounding.

(e) A background of harmonic figuration is normal to help to retain the complete sound. Plain chords do not always sound adequate as a background, and the use of arpeggios, Alberti type basses, repeated chords and broken chords are common devices.

409. The best composers to study a real piano texture in are Schumann and Chopin, and to a certain extent Beethoven.

410. In analysing the harmony of piano music, the first step is to find a true bass.

In this example, the bass changes with each melody note.

The true bass, however, may not always be on the first beat of the bar:

Bars 1 and 4 only show the true bass on the second beat of the bar. Here the bass does not change with each melody note.

411. If we reduce this to its simplest form, it is seen to be in three parts, all of which are doubled:

Beethoven: *Sonata in E♭, Op. 7*

Reduced to its simplest form.

The broken chords in the original are much more rich and sonorous than the plain chords.

412. The individual notes of any arpeggio group of notes generally follow the same horizontal laws of part-progression which would be observed if the same harmonies were written in a succession of unbroken chords.

Mendelssohn: *Lieder ohne Worte, No. 1*

Beethoven: *Rondo Grazioso. Op. 51*

The resolution, if it does not immediately follow a discord, will be found in an arpeggio group in a corresponding place to that which the discord itself occupied in the previous group.
Simplified thus:

413. Arpeggio Figures frequently have passing-notes mixed with them:

This is an example of a principal (arpeggio) part for the right hand, with a more or less defined under-current of melody for the left hand.
The following is an example of a principal melody consisting entirely of arpeggio figures in which downward-resolving appoggiaturas occur:

The left hand part can be thus simplified:

Observe that C, the discord which occurs in the middle of the second arpeggio group in the left hand, is resolved upon B, the middle note of the next group.

UPWARD-RESOLVING APPOGGIATURAS are also to be found mixed with arpeggio figures:

Beethoven: *Sonata in C minor, Op. 10, No. 1*

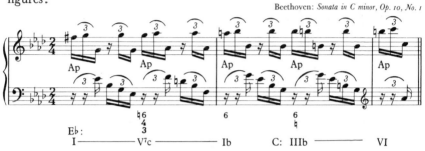

Reduced to its simplest form.

Here, it will be observed, the real bass is to be found upon the very last note of the arpeggio figure; which *is* the bass, because it is the lowest note of the *chord*.

SUSPENSIONS AND RETARDATIONS are sometimes heard mixed with arpeggio figures:

Beethoven: *Sonata in G, Op. 14, No. 2*

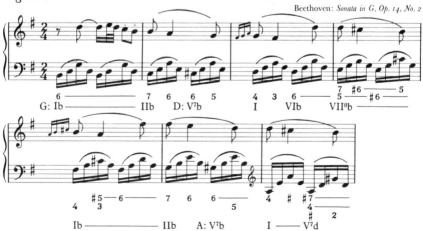

There is no difficulty here in distinguishing the principal from the accompanying part. But the retardations in the latter are not so easily recognised. They can be at once perceived, however, when the passage is reduced to its simplest form:

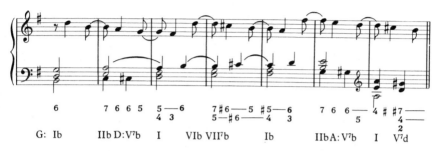

The passage is now seen to be quite an ordinary specimen of four-part harmony; it will be observed that the suspensions in the top part are admirably accompanied by the retardations in the part next below the top. Even pedal notes (direct and inverted) sometimes find their way into arpeggio figures:

414.

Beethoven: *Sonata Pathetique, Op. 13*

Here, too, there is no difficulty in distinguishing the principal from the accompanying parts. The pedal notes (tonic and dominant) will be more clearly seen when the passage is reduced to its simplest form:

415. And so, in writing piano accompaniments, the first step is to discover the basic harmony. Next, decide on a good bass line, always having regard to the points of cadence in the given melody and the style of the given example, making use of the resources discussed above.

416. In writing music for three orchestral instruments, try to keep the harmony clear by sounding the root and the third in any chord. There may be harmonic ambiguity if only the third and fifth are sounding, though contrapuntal movement may conceal it to some extent. For example, (a) is very bare, but (b) demonstrates a firm harmonic line:

Remember too to allow rests for the players to breathe and remember that the flute requires more breath than the other woodwind instruments.

THE SUITE

417. The dances of the suite.

The three fundamental dances of the suite at the end of the 17th century were Allemande, Courante and Sarabande. To these was added the Gigue as finale.

Between the Sarabande and the Gigue were introduced the "Galanteries". These were any other dances that the composer chose, and the variety in Bach's French Suites is considerable.

FUNDAMENTAL DANCES

ALLEMANDE—a stately dance in $\frac{4}{4}$, flowing in character and generally with one or three semiquaver upbeats:

COURANTE—2 types:

(a) Italian—quick $\frac{3}{4}$, running in style:

(b) French—stately $\frac{6}{4}$, changing to $\frac{3}{2}$ at the cadence. This rhythm is known as a Hemiole, or Hemiola:

SARABANDE—Stately $\frac{3}{4}$ or $\frac{9}{2}$ with a tendency toward an accent on the second beat and use of the following rhythmic pattern:

140

GIGUE—Lively dance, nearly always written in compound time, using time signatures such as 6/8, 12/8, 12/16 or 9/16. But may also be found with simple time signatures such as 3/8, C, or 2/1.

Examples from Bach:

French Suite in B minor

French Suite in E

French Suite in G

French Suite in D minor

Partita in F

Partita in D

Partita in E minor

GALANTERIES

MINUET.—Stately dance in triple time. Often a second minuet was added and the first one repeated afterwards. This repeat is not always written out, but is indicated by the words "Minuet da capo" or simply "da capo" written at the end of the second minuet. This last is often known as the TRIO, a name derived from the fact that in earlier times it was played by a trio of two oboes and bassoon in the ballets of Lully. The other dances were often provided with trios in the same way in their own styles and rhythms.

A minuet may have more than one trio, for example that in Mozart's *Clarinet quintet*.

AIR.—Any flowing piece, generally not too fast and of a melodic character.

ANGLAISE.—A quick dance in $\frac{2}{2}$ commencing on the first beat of the bar. Compare Bourrée.

GAVOTTE.—A stately dance in $\frac{2}{2}$ beginning on the second beat of the bar.

MUSETTE.—Often acts as a trio to the Gavotte and derives its name from its drone bass which resembles the drone of the bagpipes, known formerly as musette.

BOURRÉE.—A quick dance in $\frac{2}{2}$ commencing on the 4th ♩ of the bar.

LOURE.—A stately dance in compound duple time.

POLONAISE.—A gentle flowing dance of Polish origin in $\frac{3}{4}$. Not the brilliant swaggering dance that Chopin wrote.

PASSEPIED.—A Breton nautical dance in triple time, generally fairly lively.

OTHER DANCES

CHACONNE.—A stately dance in $\frac{3}{4}$ with an accent on the second beat and often built on a ground bass (i.e. a bass that repeats itself throughout a piece).

PASSACAGLIA.—A fairly stately dance generally (but not always) in triple time and usually built on a ground bass.

SICILIANO.—A pastoral dance in $\frac{6}{8}$, but always "con moto". Often used for vocal pieces, for example "He shall feed his flock" by Handel (*Messiah*).

PAVAN OR PAVANE.—A stately Spanish dance originally in common time but latterly often in triple time. This was often followed by—

GALLIARD.—A lively triple time dance.

RIGAUDON.—A fast common time dance with occasionally a vocal accompaniment.

HORNPIPE.—A nautical dance generally in common time, but there are specimens in a variety of time signatures.

MODERN AND NATIONAL DANCE FORMS

MAZURKA.—A national Polish dance, in $\frac{3}{4}$ or $\frac{3}{8}$ time, with often a strong accent on the second beat of the bar.

TARANTELLA.—A lively Neapolitan dance, in $\frac{6}{8}$ time, in which a continuous flow of even triplets is maintained.

SALTARELLO (Latin: *saltare* "to jump").—A popular Roman dance, generally in the minor key, $\frac{12}{8}$ time, in the rhythm of which the jumping or hopping step is apparent:

REEL.—A very quick dance, more particularly belonging to Scotland.

SEGUIDILLA.—A Spanish dance in triple time, accompanied by singing and by castanets.

FANDANGO.—Another Spanish dance, with castanet accompaniment, somewhat resembling the Seguidilla, but it is slower, and in $\frac{6}{8}$ time.

BOLERO.—A Spanish dance in triple time, with castanets, performed by only two persons.

VALSE or WALTZ.—A well-known dance in triple time, $\frac{3}{4}$ or $\frac{3}{8}$.

GALOP.—A quick dance in $\frac{2}{4}$ time.

POLKA.—A lively dance, of Bohemian origin, in $\frac{2}{4}$ time, with a strong accent upon the third quaver.

SCHOTTISCHE.—A dance of German origin, written in $\frac{2}{4}$ time.

A PRELUDE is an introductory piece which precedes a longer or more important movement, such as a fugue. Its form is not fixed, but is *variable*, being sometimes in simple binary, and sometimes in freer form. It is often developed from a short melodic phrase, section, or motive. It is generally complete in itself—that is, it comes to a full close in its own key.

An INTRODUCTION is a movement of even less definite design than the prelude. It is incomplete in itself, and leads without a break into the fugue or other movement which it is intended to "introduce"; being merely intended to excite the attention and interest of the listeners for what is to come.

TOCCATA.—This is a kind of Prelude in which a certain passage or figure is elaborately developed either in the Strict or the Free Style. Toccata is derived from the Italian verb *toccare*, "to touch". It is essentially a piece for showing the "touch" or executive skill of the performer. For examples of movements in Toccata style see Beethoven's *Sonata VI in F*, Op. 10, No. 2 (last movement); *Sonata XII in A flat*, Op. 26 (last movement); *Sonata XXII in F*, Op. 54 (last movement); Bach's *Prelude in B flat*, Book I of the "48".

But note that in the 17th century Frescobaldi wrote Toccatas for performance during the most solemn moments of the celebration of the Mass, which were slow improvisatory pieces.

MUSICAL FORMS

418. The word "Form" applied to music is generally taken to mean the structure or plan of a piece having regard to:

(a) the arrangement of themes

(b) the design of the key relationships.

419. Many of the dances mentioned above fall into what is called BINARY or OPEN form; binary because it is basically in two parts, open because the first half, ending in a related key, is incomplete and requires the second part to complete it:

Its key plan is that described in paragraphs 263–4 and 306–7.

A binary form may be a simple one like the Sarabande in Bach's *E major French Suite* or a considerably extended piece containing several themes or ideas as in some of the longer Bach movements or the sonatas of Scarlatti.

420. The first half of a binary form often ends with a double bar and both halves may be repeated.

The second half is often much longer than the first. Bach's *D major Prelude* in the 2nd book of the "48 Preludes and Fugues" is an example. In this, the second half commences with the same theme as the opening, but in the dominant key and modulates widely before returning to the tonic, where the themes of the opening half return, all in the tonic key. This will show the proportions of the piece:

Keys:	D-A	A-modulations-D	
Number of bars:	16 bars	:‖: 24 bars	16 bars

The style of the movement is consistent throughout.

421. When the structure described above is expanded by introducing two sets of contrasted ideas into the first half, one in the tonic and the other in the related key, a movement with much more dramatic tension results. This is briefly the principle of SONATA FORM or FIRST MOVEMENT FORM.

The first half of this is known as the EXPOSITION. The two sets of contrasted ideas are known as 1st and 2nd SUBJECTS, or 1st and 2nd GROUPS respectively. The word "Group" is more accurate since often a large number of ideas is involved, but the term Subject is in such universal use that, so long as a group of ideas is understood by it, there can be no harm in using it.

The two subjects generally have a linking passage between them designed to effect a firm modulation from the first key to the second. This is called BRIDGE PASSAGE or TRANSITION.

The long second half commences with modulations and is known as the DEVELOPMENT or FREE FANTASIA section. Its purpose is to make inevitable a return to the tonic key as the climax of the piece. The return to the tonic is often achieved over a dominant pedalpoint.

The final section is known as the RECAPITULATION, and in it the two subject groups are repeated, but this time all in the tonic key. This obviously involves a change in the transition or bridge passage since no modulation is required.

There may or may not be a CODA to bring the movement to a close. Note that the coda of Beethoven's *Sonata Op. 81a* is longer than the development and the recapitulation put together.

422. The design may be summarised thus:

Exposition	{ 1st Subject group	Key 1
	{ Transition	Modulations
	{ 2nd Subject group	Key 2
Development	— —	Various
Recapitulation	{ 1st Subject group	Key 1
	{ Transition (altered)	—
	{ 2nd Subject group	Key 1
Coda	— —	Various, but mainly key 1

423. In the slow movements of many classical sonatas this form is used in a shortened version by omitting the development, in which case the exposition runs straight into the recapitulation with possibly a few chords as a link. This is generally known as MODIFIED SONATA FORM. An example is to be found in the 2nd movement of Beethoven's *Sonata in C minor*, Op. 10, No. 1.

424. The other basic form for small movements is known as TERNARY or CLOSED form—ternary because it is in 3 parts of which the 3rd is generally a repeat of the first; closed because the 1st section ends in the tonic key and is complete in itself. An example is to be found in any Scherzo-trio-scherzo structure.

The middle section is known as an EPISODE. After the repeat of the first section there may be a coda which, in the case of Schubert's well-known *Impromptu in E flat*, uses the thematic material of the middle episode.

This is the form in which many short pieces are written such as the Mazurkas of Chopin; it is also found not uncommonly among the movements of sonatas. Any dance which has a trio and is then repeated comes under this heading, even though the individual minuet or trio may be a binary structure. This form may conveniently be described as ABA form.

425. If this ternary form is extended by the addition of further episodes, interspersed with repeats of the main section, the resulting structure is known as RONDO. There is no limit to the number of episodes possible, and among the keyboard works of Couperin are many examples with episodes running into double figures. These were known as COUPLETS in Couperin's works. In the classical sonata, a rondo normally consists of two episodes sandwiched between appearances of the main theme—ABACA. Note that A will be in the tonic at each appearance, B and C being in related keys. Example, Beethoven *Sonata in G*, finale, Op. 79.

Note that rondo form is used commonly in slow movements too, in which case the different sections will probably be short and may run into one another. The name EPISODICAL form is sometimes used for a rondo.

426. In large finales in the classical sonatas and symphonies, the rondo is frequently further extended by repeating the 1st episode again in the tonic and following it with yet another appearance of the main theme. This is known as SONATA RONDO or RONDO SONATA or MODERN RONDO or even NEW RONDO. It may be conveniently described as follows:

	A	B	A	C	A	B	A	Coda
Keys	1	2	1	3	1	1	1	

This is obviously a big-scale movement and is common in Beethoven. Examples:

Sonatas   Op. 2, No. 2 finale
Op. 2, No. 3 finale
Op. 7 finale
Op. 13 finale—a very concise one

427. The central episode "C" of the sonata rondo may be a development of previously heard material instead of an independent episode. Two of the best examples of this are to be found in the second movement of Beethoven's *Sonata in E minor*, Op. 90 and in the finale of Op. 27, No. 1. The latter approaches very closely to sonata form proper in style and omits the final repeat of the main theme, adding instead a coda.

428. Rondo style and Sonata form style differ in that the former is broad, leisurely and melodic, with a certain squareness and symmetry in phrase shape, while the latter is much more terse and pithy with more short ideas, and is consequently more dramatic.

429. The Classical sonata considered as a complete work.

The normal series of movements in the classical sonata is:

1. a quick movement in sonata form.

2. a slow movement in ternary, rondo, modified sonata or other simple form.

Examples of sonata form and sonata rondo are not so common in slow movements since they obviously occupy more space, but there are plenty of examples to be discovered among large scale works.

3. Finale, a quick movement in rondo, sonata rondo or sonata form.

1 and 3 are in the tonic key, 2 may be in any related key, often the subdominant. To the above 3 movements a minuet and trio (which in the hands of Haydn became a scherzo and trio) are often added between 2 and 3.

430. Symphonies and chamber music of the period follow the same structural principles.

431. The Sonata of the period before 1750 was different. The style of the music was contrapuntal and the sonata, known as TRIO SONATA, was written for three instruments, two melodic and a bass, all supported by a harmonic background: this was played on a keyboard instrument, generally the harpsichord, and was known as CONTINUO.

The continuo player played from a bass line with the harmonies indicated by the figures we have already encountered in discussing chord positions, 6, $\frac{6}{4}$, 7, $\frac{6}{5}$, etc. Generally he had to improvise, and the art of doing this became a highly developed skill in the Baroque period.

432. The sonatas were normally four movements—slow, quick, slow, quick and two distinct styles emerged in the 17th century, the SONATA DA CHIESA, severe and serious for church use, and the SONATA DA CAMERA, much lighter in style and with its movements more like dances.

433. When composers like Bach wrote sonatas for one solo instrument, together with bass and continuo, they often dispensed with the opening slow movement. The structure thus resembles the 3-movement overture of Italian opera in the early eighteenth century.

434. The early CONCERTI GROSSI were really sonatas for orchestra. The division of the players into a small group of soloists known as the CONCERTINO and a large group known as RIPIENO produced echo effects and changes of dynamic level. This is the style in which Torelli and Corelli wrote and also Handel in the String Concerti, Op. 6.

435. The solo concerti of Albinoni and Vivaldi introduce a new principle into the concerto, known as the RITORNELLO PRINCIPLE. The opening paragraph of the movement is given generally to the ripieno alone, this paragraph being known as the ritornello. A much greater contrast between ripieno and concertino is made and the passages of concertino are framed by appearances of the ritornello or by portions of it so that the course of the movement is roughly as follows:

Ritornello (Ripieno) Tonic	Solo (Concertino) Tonic—1st related key	Ritornello in 1st related key	Solo from 1st related key to 2nd	Ritornello in 2nd related key	Solo from 2nd related key to 1st	Ritornello in Tonic

Modulation takes place in the Solo or Concertino passages, and here the ripieno instruments are used to accompany the Concertino. The Concertino may or may not use the same melodic ideas as the ripieno.

436. This same Ritornello Principle is also exemplified in many of the Arias in Operas and Cantatas of Bach's and Handel's period. An example is the "Quoniam" in Bach's Mass in B Minor, where the orchestral Ritornello occurs in D major, A major, B minor and finally, in D major. Not every appearance of it is complete. This kind of structure is sometimes called ARIA FORM.

437. The concerti of Mozart and Beethoven apply this ritornello principle to movements in sonata form and rondo:

Ritornello—Exposition—Ritornello—Development—

Ritornello—Recapitulation—Ritornello.

The applications to rondo are too varied to give a definite plan, but as long as it is remembered that the ritornello marks the ends of sections, analysis is fairly straightforward. But the returns of rondo main themes are often amalgamated with ritornelli, thus obviating over-much repetition.

438. This Ritornello Form also appears in movements which are obviously composed for a harpsichord with two contrasting manuals. Examples of this are to be found scattered among Bach's keyboard works. Two obvious ones are the first and third movements of his "Italian Concerto", also the first movement of his "English Suite" in G minor.

439. FUGUE is a contrapuntal texture in which each voice enters with the principal theme, known as the SUBJECT, in turn. EPISODES, modulating to other keys, link up entries of the subject in those keys, the whole composition going through a cycle of keys on the same lines as the general design followed by simple dance movements. The first section introduces the participating voices, the middle section moves through various keys and the final section is marked by the return to the tonic key with the reappearance of the subject therein:

	1st Section	Middle Section			Final Sec.
	Entry in turn of all voices	Episode	Entries of subject	Episode	Subject in 1
Keys	1	Modulating	2	Modulating	1

This is only a sketch plan; the number of episodes and entries of the subject may be extended considerably in the middle section, and there are many fugues which are difficult to fit into any prescribed form. So it is best to think of fugue as a special way of writing, a special kind of contrapuntal texture, rather than try and force it into a rigid scheme.

440. The following terms are met with in fugue:

(a) COUNTER SUBJECT. The counterpoint with which the first voice accompanies the second if it also reappears with subsequent appearances of the subject:

J. S. Bach: *Fugue in G minor Bk. 1 Op. 48*

(b) ANSWER. The 1st section of the fugue introduces the voices in turn, the second voice to enter answers the first in or on the dominant. There are two kinds of answer:

(i) REAL ANSWER. The second voice enters with an exact transposition of the subject:

J. S. Bach: *Fugue in D minor, Bk. 1 Op. 48*

(ii) TONAL ANSWER. The second voice frequently enters with a modified version of the subject. This is a complex matter and cannot be dealt with in detail here; the general principle is that in answering subject with answer, the tonic must be answered with the dominant and the dominant with the tonic *in the first few notes of the subject*.

J. S. Bach: *Fugue in G minor Bk. 1 Op. 48*

A subject that modulates to the dominant must have an answer that modulates back to the tonic:

J. S. Bach: *Fugue in E♭, Bk. 1 Op. 48*

Ans.

(c) CODETTA. An episodical link during the first section between entries, most commonly between 2nd and 3rd entries:

J. S. Bach: *Fugue in G minor, Bk. 1 Op. 48*

(d) AUGMENTATION. The notes of the subject in longer note values. Similarly:

(e) DIMINUTION. The notes of the subject in shorter note values.

(f) INVERSION. The intervals of the subject inverted. This subject has already been explained.

(g) MIDDLE ENTRIES. The entries of the subject or answer in the middle section of the fugue, generally in keys other than the tonic.

(h) STRETTO. Two or more overlapping entries of the subject, the 2nd commencing before the 1st has finished.

J. S. Bach: *Fugue in G minor, Bk. 1 Op. 48*

In this example, there is stretto for three voices showing augmentation in the alto and inversion in the tenor:

S. in soprano   J. S. Bach: *Fugue in C minor, Bk. II, Op. 48*

Inversion in tenor

A stretto involving all the voices of a fugal texture is known as STRETTO MAESTRALE:

J. S. Bach: *Fugue in B♭ minor, Bk. I, Op. 48*

(i) DOUBLE FUGUE. A fugue on two subjects which may be announced together at the outset, or separately and combined at a later stage. Example: *G sharp minor Fugue* in Book II of the "48".

(j) TRIPLE FUGUE. A fugue on 3 subjects. Example: *C sharp minor Fugue* in Book I of the "48".

441.   That fugue is not really a musical form but a kind of texture, a way of writing, that has a very special rhetorical effect is demonstrated by its use in other structures in music, notably Sonata Form. Here, its effect is to hold up progress, to create tension and, consequently, to prepare for a climax. This becomes a feature of the writing in Beethoven's later works. Both the transition and the development of his last Sonata for piano are in fugue, and the development of the Ninth Symphony is a huge triple fugue which creates the tension that prepares the movement's recapitulation.

So it is better to speak of a piece as being "in fugue" than to say it is "a fugue".

442. The OVERTURE in the 17th and 18th centuries was of two basic types:
(a) The FRENCH OVERTURE as found in Lully, Handel, Purcell and
others consists of a slow pompous introduction using a sharply dotted
rhythm, followed by a fugue in quicker time. The slow introduction
was occasionally repeated after the fugue.
(b) The ITALIAN OVERTURE as found in the operas of Alessandro
Scarlatti, Vivaldi and others was in three movements, fast-slow-fast,
and was the precursor of the classical symphony.
The classical concert overture is a movement in some kind of sonata
form. Examples: Beethoven, *Coriolan* , *Egmont*, *Leonora No. 3*, etc.

443. VARIATIONS may be grouped under several headings:
(a) Ground bass, in which the bass line persists throughout, while
above it the music develops freely. Many examples in Purcell, e.g.
Dido's Lament.
Many of the grounds are of dance origin, when the phrasing of the
music follows the shape of the ground bass. Example: Corelli, *La folia*.
(b) A basic harmonic progression is the framework for each variation.
Examples: Bach, *Goldberg Variations*, Beethoven, *Diabelli Variations*.
(c) Melodic, in which the melody is subjected to decoration. Many
examples in the slow movements of Beethoven's Sonatas, e.g. Op.
14, No. 2, Op. 57, etc.
A special form of this is "Air et Doubles" in which the doubles,
another word for variations, become progressively more complex
and rapid in note movement. Example: Handel, in the Suite in
E major—a set known as "*The Harmonious Blacksmith*", also the slow
movement of Beethoven's *Sonatas, Op. 57 and Op. 111.*
(d) Variations where an idea from the theme is used in the composition of each piece, but where the basic shape of the original theme is
not followed. Example: Elgar, Enigma Variations. Tovey used to
call these, variations where the composer did not know his theme.

444. Other forms of composition developed in the seventeenth and
eighteenth centuries.

445. The CHORAL or CHORALE PRELUDE is one. Like the fugue, it is difficult
to lay down any rules for its structure, so varied is its treatment of its material.
Among the composers who wrote Chorale Preludes are Sweelinck, Pachelbel,
Buxtehude, Reinken, Bohm and, of course, J. S. Bach. Bach's Chorale
Preludes are basically of two types, firstly a plain elaboration of the harmonisation of the Chorale without its losing its rhythmic shape, and secondly,
the CHORALE FANTASIA where each line of the Chorale is introduced by and
accompanied by a passage of contrapuntal texture, resulting in a fairly
extensive composition. Examples of the former are to be found in the
"Orgelbüchlein" or Little Organ Book, while examples of the latter are to
be found in the collection known as "The Eighteen" as well as elsewhere.

446. The CANON. Again this is not to be thought of as being in any specific form. It is a texture in which each voice imitates exactly the previous one to enter. ROUNDS and CATCHES are forms of infinitely repeating Canons. If the Canon is for two voices, it is known as Canon 2 in 1. If it is for four voices, it is Canon 4 in 1, provided that each voice has the same melody. If there are two complementary melodies a four voice is 4 in 2. The first voice to lead off is known as "Dux", the imitating voices are known as "Comes". Canons may demonstrate augmentation, diminution, inversion etc. in the Comes. Examples of Canon: Every third variation of Bach's "Goldberg Variations" is a canon, and Schumann's Op. 56 is a set of canons for pedal piano. Canon is commom in episodes of fugal pieces.

447. Nineteenth century music tends to develop new ideas which as often as not are grafted on to Classical structures. The "Unity in Diversity" principle of the Classical symphonic style is, to some extent, discarded and a more obvious unity through thematic resemblance becomes an important principle.

448. Berlioz invented a theme which recurs in all the movements of his Symphonie Fantastique which he calls an IDÉE FIXE. This is even caricatured in the last movement which is entitled "A Witch's Sabbath".

449. The term "Thematic Metamorphosis" or transformation of themes is used to describe the proceedings of Liszt. His piano Sonata in B minor is a good example of this principle. Here three basic ideas provide the main themes in both fast and slow tempi, and also provide much of the accompaniment figuration. The Sonata is in one very big sonata form with many transformations and changes of tempo.

450. Brahms' second Symphony has a number of themes in all four of the movements which are derived from the opening of the first movement as a kind of "Germ".

451. PROGRAMME MUSIC is a prominent nineteenth century principle. The afore-mentioned Symphonie Fantastique of Berlioz is an example. Its movements all have descriptive titles and the Symphony has a descriptive programme. Arising out of this, the SYMPHONIC POEM and TONE POEM appear, descriptive structures, as often as not built on the Sonata Form principle, but illustrating a story or describing an idea or a mood. Examples are; Liszt, Les Preludes, Prometheus, A Faust Symphony; Richard Strauss, Don Juan and Sibelius, Tapiola.

452. The association of themes with persons or ideas or events reaches its logical climax in OPERA, especially in Wagner, whose use of LEITMOTIVEN allowed him to build whole acts of operas with symphonic continuity and coherence.

453. A new constructive principle is demonstrated by Sibelius whose symphonic movements tend to be built on a series of germinal ideas until, at the climax, a new theme appears. A good example is the first movement of his Fifth Symphony in E flat.

454. Songs are often grouped into SONG CYCLES where each one is connected to the following one in subject matter, story, and in key relationship. Examples are: Beethoven, "An die ferne Geliebte" and Schumann, "Frauenliebe und-leben".

455. As the nineteenth century draws to a close, the intense chromaticisation of the harmony tends to undermine tonality, and a new principle appears—ATONALITY, or lack of key centre. From this, Schoenberg especially, but others too, develop SERIALISM. This is a way of composing through preserving an arbitrarily chosen order of the 12 notes of the chromatic scale throughout a piece. This series of notes is known as a TONE ROW. Later experiments with this have involved attempts to unify all the parameters of pitch, intensity, rhythm, etc. by relating them to the proportions implied by the intervals of the original Tone Row.

456. The use of exotic scales and rhythms is a prominent feature of the music of a number of composers, notably Bartok and Messaien. And so we go on experimenting with new ideas.

APPENDIX

MUSICAL TERMS AND DIRECTIONS FOR PERFORMANCE

WORDS SHOWING STRENGTH OF TONE:

Pianissimo (pp), very soft.
Mezzo piano (mp), moderately soft.
Piano (p), soft.
Mezza voce (mv), medium tone.
Mezzo forte (mf), moderately loud.
Forte f, loud.
Fortissimo (ff), very loud.
Crescendo or $\underline{\qquad}$, gradually becoming louder.
Decrescendo
Diminuendo } or $\underline{\qquad}$, gradually becoming softer.
Sforzando (sf)
Forzando (fz) }, accented.
Rinforzando (rf), strengthening the tone.

WORDS SHOWING SPEED:

Grave, extremely slow, solemn.
Lento, slow.
Largo, broad.
Larghetto, rather broad.
Adagio, slow, leisurely.
Andante, going at an easy pace.
Andantino, at a moderate pace, but not so slow as *andante*.
Moderato, moderate speed.
Allegretto, rather fast.
Allegro, fast.
Vivace, lively.
Presto, very quick.
Prestissimo, very quick indeed, as fast as possible.

The following other words relating to speed are also often met with:

Accelerando (accel.), getting gradually faster.
Rallentando (rall.), getting gradually slower.
Calando, softer and slower.
Ritardando (ritard., rit.), retarding the speed.
Ritenuto (riten.), held back.
A tempo, in time.
Ad libitum (ad lib.) or *A piacere*, at the performer's pleasure.
Meno mosso, slower at once.
Più mosso, quicker at once.

The signs > and ∧ are called ACCENTS, and are used to mark strongly accented notes.

Terms relating to Tone:

Mancando, failing or waning tone.
Smorzando ⎱
Morendo ⎰ , dying away.
Piu forte, more loudly.
Piu piano, more softly.
Meno forte, less loudly.
Meno piano, less softly.
Perdendosi, losing itself by getting softer and slower.

Terms relating to Speed:

Largamente, broadly, massively.
Adagietto, rather leisurely.
Tempo ordinario, ordinary speed.
Tempo commodo, convenient, *i.e.* comfortable speed.
Vivacissimo, extremely lively.
Tosto, quick; rapid.
Celere, quick; nimble.
Veloce, swiftly.
Stringendo (string.) ⎫
Stretto ⎬ , pressing onwards, hurrying the speed.
Affrettando ⎭
Tempo Giusto, in strict, or *exact* time.
Doppio Tempo, or *Doppio Movimento,* in double time, *i.e.* twice as fast as the preceding movement.
L'istesso tempo, in the same time as the preceding movement. This term is used when the time signature is changed, but the *beats* are still to be of the same length as before.
Tempo Primo, at the same speed as at first.
Piu lento, more slowly.

ITALIAN WORDS INDICATING EXPRESSION, ETC.

Agitato	In an agitated manner.
Animato	Animated.
Appassionato	Impassioned.
Cantabile; Cantando ...	In a singing style.
Capriccioso	Fanciful; capricious.
Con anima	With soul, *i.e.,* life.
Con brio	With vivacity, brilliance.
Con espressione	With expression.
Con energia	With energy or force.
Con fuoco	With fire.
Con grazia	With grace.
Con moto	With motion, *i.e.,* rather fast.
Con spirito	With spirit.
Con tenerezza	With tenderness.
Deciso	Decided, *i.e.,* with firmness.
Delicato	Delicately; refined.

Dolce	...	...	... Sweetly, gently.
Energico	...	...	... In an energetic manner.
Espressivo	...	...	... Expressively.
Forza	...	...	... Force or emphasis.
Furioso	...	...	... Impetuously; with fury.
Giusto	...	...	... Right; exact; strict.
Grandioso	...	...	... Grandly.
Grazioso	...	...	... Gracefully; daintily.
Legato	...	...	... Smoothly and connectedly.
Leggiero	...	...	... Lightly.
Maestoso	...	...	... Majestic.
Marcato	...	...	... Marked.
Martellato	...	...	... With great force; hammered.
Mesto	...	...	... In a pensive, sad manner.
Mosso	...	...	... Moved, *i.e.*, fast.
Pesante	...	...	... Heavily; in a ponderous manner.
Piacevole	...	...	... In a pleasing manner.
Pomposo	...	...	... Pompously.
Risoluto	...	...	... In a resolute manner.
Rubato	...	...	... Robbed (flexible in time) see tempo rubato.
Scherzando; Scherzoso		...	In a sprightly, playful manner.
Semplice	...	...	... Simply.
Serioso	...	...	... Seriously.
Sonore	...	...	... Sonorous.
Sostenuto	...	...	... Sustained.
Sotto voce	...	...	... In a subdued manner; in an *undertone*.

Tempo rubato ... ... { Robbed time; the slight alterations by acceleration or retardation which a performer makes for the purpose of expression.

Teneramente }
Con tenerezza } ... ... Tenderly.

Tranquillo ... ... Tranquilly.

Vivo; Con vivacita ... ... With vivacity.

ITALIAN ADJECTIVES, PREPOSITIONS, ETC., USED BEFORE OTHER WORDS

A ...	...	...	... At; for; with; to; by; in.
Al, All', Alla	...	...	In the style of; to the.
Assai	...	...	... Very, fairly.
Bene or *Ben*	...	...	Well.
Con	...	...	... With.
Da	...	...	... From.
Dal	...	...	... From the; *Dal segno*, from the sign.

Di	...	Of the.
Il or *La*	...	The.
Ma	...	But.
Meno	...	Less.
Mezzo	...	Half.
Molto or *Di molto*	...	Much; very much.
Non	...	Not.
O	...	Either; or.
Piu	...	More.
Pochettino	...	Very little.
Poco or *Un poco* ...	...	A little.
Quasi	...	Almost; as it were; as if.
Sempre	...	Always.
Senza	...	Without.
Sul' ; *Sull'* ; *Sulla* ...	...	On the.
Tanto	...	As much.
Troppo	...	Too; too much.
Un or *Una* ...	...	A; an; one.

The above words are often found in conjunction with the other words already listed. Examples of these compound terms are:

Allegro animato ...	...	Quick; animated.
Allegro commodo ...	...	A convenient *Allegro*—comfortably fast.
Allegro con anima ...	...	Quick, with life (spirit).
Allegro con fuoco ...	...	Quick, with fire.
Allegro moderato ...	...	Moderately quick.
Allegro molto ...	...	Very quick.
Allegro non tanto ...	...	Not so quick.
Allegro non troppo ...	...	Not too quick.
Allegro vivace ...	...	Lively and brisk.
Poco a poco cres. ...	...	Getting louder little by little.
Andante con moto ...	...	A trifle faster than *Andante* alone.
Andante quasi Allegretto	...	Faster than *Andante*, almost as if *Allegretto*.
Ben marcato ...	...	Well marked.
Meno allegro ...	...	Less quick.
Sempre più crescendo ...	...	Continually increasing in tone.
Presto assai ...	...	Very quick.

ITALIAN WORDS CONVEYING GENERAL DIRECTIONS TO THE PERFORMER

Bis (*Italian and Latin*) ... Twice. Short passages, such as a single bar or two bars which are to be played or sung twice, have the Latin word *Bis* (*i.e.*, twice) written over or under a slur, so:

Come	Like; as; how.
Come prima	As at first.
Come sopra	As above.
Da Capo	'From the beginning.' When the term *Da Capo* or *D.C.* occurs at any part of a piece, it signifies that the music is to be repeated from the beginning.
Da Capo al fine	From the beginning to the word *Fine*.
Da Capo al Segno	From the beginning to the sign %.
Da Capo senza ripetizione ...	From the beginning, without repetition.
Dal Segno	From the sign %.
Fine	The end. A pause when placed over a double bar in the middle of a piece means that the piece is to end there, after a *Da Capo*. The word *Fine* is frequently used for this purpose instead of the pause:
Pedal or ped. (English) ...	In ORGAN MUSIC this word is used to indicate the notes to be played by the Organist's feet. In PIANO MUSIC it indicates that the *right* pedal is to be pressed down with the foot, and kept in that position until the * (or a change of harmony) occurs, when the pedal should be raised. The words *Senza sordini* are generally understood in piano music to mean 'without dampers' (*i.e.*, with a free use of the right pedal); and *Con sordini* to mean 'with dampers' (*i.e.*, without the right pedal). In modern music the words *Una Corda* indicate the use of the left pedal; and the words *Tre Corde* show where it should be raised. The student must not confuse the two words *mutes* and *dampers*. A mute is any contrivance for merely decreasing the average intensity of a sound; a damper is a piece of mechanism which stops the vibration of the sound-producing apparatus, and so causes actual silence.
Poco a poco	Little by little

Repeat marks	Dots when written *before* a Double-bar indicate that the music is to be repeated from the previous Double-bar, or from the beginning of the piece: Dots when placed *after* a Double-bar indicate that the music to the following Double-bar is to be repeated: Repeat marks, such as the above, are used only for *long* passages intended for Repetition. For short passages of a bar or so, the word *Bis* is used.

R.H. and *L.H.* ... ...

These letters indicate the use of the Right Hand or Left Hand in piano music:

Mano Destra (It.)	...	...	M.D. =R.H.
Mano Sinistra (It.)	...	...	M.S. =L.H.
Main Droite (Fr.)	...	...	M.D. =R.H.
Maine Gauche (Fr.)	...	...	M.G. =L.H.

are also used for the same purpose.

Segno ... ... A sign *Al Segno* means 'to the sign'. *Dal Segno* 'from the sign'.

Simile ... ... In the same manner.

Tenuto—Ten ... ... Held or *sustained*

Volta ... ... Turn; time. The signs 1*ma volta* (1st time) and 2*da volta* (2nd time), or simply the figures 1 and 2, are often used in conjunction with Repeats; the Bar or Bars marked 1 are then to be omitted at the Repetition, and the Bar or Bars marked 2 played instead:

Volti Subito—V.S. ... Turn over quickly to the next page.

The METRONOME is an instrument invented by Maelzel to measure accurately the *speed* of a piece of music. It is worked by clockwork, which controls a pendulum as in a clock, except that the pendulum of a Metronome is fixed at its lower end, instead of at the top as in a clock. On this pendulum is a sliding weight, and behind it is a scale marked in figures. The pendulum beats so many times in a minute, according to the figure to which the sliding weight is set. If the weight is set to the figure 60, the pendulum will beat 60 times in a minute, that is, once a second.

If, for example, we see the 'metronome mark' $\quad =126$, it means that the sliding weight should be set at the figure 126, when the pendulum, on being set in motion, will show the speed of the Crotchets—126 in a minute. Similarly, $\quad =80$ means that the weight is to be set at 80, and the pendulum beats will show the speed of the Minims—80 to a minute.

SUPPLEMENTARY LIST OF ITALIAN TERMS

Affetto	With affection.
Affettuoso	With tender feeling.
Alla Capella	In the style of unaccompanied church music.
Amabile	Amiably.
Amoroso	Lovingly.
Ancora	Again.
Ardito	With spirit and boldness.
Arioso	A short melody.
Attacca	Go on immediately.
Barcarola	A boat-song.
Burlesco	Comic; funny.
Cadenza	A florid, ornamental passage, generally intended as a means of technical display.
Cantilena	A song-like melody.
Col, Colla	With the.
Col arco	With the bow (stringed instruments).
Colla parte; colla voce ...	The accompanist to keep closely with the solo part, or voice.
Come prima	As at first.
Con amore	Lovingly.
Con delicatezza	With delicacy; in a refined manner.
Con dolore; con duolo ...	With grief.
Con sordini	With mutes. In *old* piano music this meant 'to release the right pedal'; in *modern* piano music, it *sometimes* means 'to use the *left* pedal'. In ORCHESTRAL MUSIC *mutes* are sometimes used to damp or deaden the sound of Violins, Horns, Trumpets and Trombones. When these are required in performance, the direction *con sordini* is placed above the part so to be played; when they are to be removed the contrary direction, *senza sordini* is given.

Di bravura ...	...	...	In a florid style; brilliantly.
Di chiaro ...	...	...	Clearly.
Di nuovo ...	...	...	Anew; again.
Divisi	...	...	Divided (largely used in orchestral music).
Dolente; doloroso ...		...	With grief.
Dopo	...	...	After.
E poi	...	...	And then.
Feroce	...	...	Fiercely.
Giocoso	...	...	Jocosely; humorously.
Giojoso	...	...	Mirthful; joyous.
Gustoso	...	...	Tastefully.
Impetuoso ...	...	...	Impetuously.
Lagrimoso ...	...	...	Tearfully; mournfully.
Languido ...	...	...	Languid.
Leggieramente	...	...	Getting gradually lighter.
Maggiore ...	...	...	Major key.
Marcia	...	...	A march.
Menuetto	...	...	A Minuet.
Minore	...	...	Minor key.
Moto	...	...	Movement, as in Andante con moto.
Nei, Nel, Nell', Nella, Nelle,			
Nello	...	...	In the.
Obbligato (Obb.) ...		...	Indispensable; some part which cannot be omitted in performance.
Ostinato	...	...	Continuous; persisted in.
Parlando; parlante		...	In a speaking manner.
Pastorale	...	...	In a pastoral style.
Pizzicato (pizz.) ...		...	Plucked. Direction to string player to pluck the strings instead of playing them with the bow.
Poi	...	...	Then.
Questo	...	...	This.
Scherzo	...	...	A playful piece.
Sciolto	...	...	Free; unrestrained.
Segue	...	...	'Then follows', *i.e.*, go on with what comes next.
Sentimento	...	...	Sentiment.
Sino	...	...	Up to; as far as; until. *D.C. sin' al segno* therefore means 'from the beginning as far as the sign'.
Si replica ...	...	...	To be repeated.
Sordino	...	...	A mute (of a stringed instrument).
Spianato	...	...	Without pathos; smooth; even; calm.
Staccatissimo		...	As short as possible.
Staccato	...	...	Short.
Strepitoso ...	...	...	In a loud, boisterous manner.
Sul G, D, or A	...	...	On the G, D, or A string of a Violin.
Sul ponticello	...	...	Play near the bridge (Violin).
Tacet	...	...	Be silent.

Tedesca	...	...	In a German manner.
Tema	...	...	A theme, generally for Variations.
Tempo di (Menuetto)		...	In the time of (a Minuet).
Trio	...	...	The central section of a three part design where the first part normally returns after the Trio. The first section may well be a Minuet or a Scherzo. Trio may also be a piece for three instruments or voices. This was the origin of the term.
Tutti	...	...	All; every performer is to take his part.
Variazione		...	Variations. See para. 443.
Vigoroso	...	...	Vigorously.
Volante	...	...	In a light, flying manner.

INDEX

(Figures refer to paragraphs unless otherwise stated)